The Yootha Joyce Scrapbook

Paul Curran

First Published by Mossy Books

mossybooks@gmail.com

Copyright © Paul Curran, 2015

A CIP catalogue record for this book is available from the British Library.

ISBN-13: 978-1506148151

ISBN-10: 1506148158

For Sarah

The Yootha Joyce Scrapbook

Acknowledgements

My sincere thanks to all the kind people who helped me compile this book. They include Fabian and Rosy Hamilton, the late Adrianne Hamilton, and David Simpson at the palacetheatreclub.org.uk, Westcliff-on-Sea, for helping me unearth details on Yootha's early theatrical appearances. In particular, I would like to thank Terence Lee Dickson for kindly agreeing to meet me recently and share his memories of Yootha, helping to put the last years of her life into perspective, and bringing her further to life. Thanks, too, for support from Christine Pilgrim, Brian Murphy, Peter Rankin and Joy Jameson; and to Mandy Carr. Thanks to Richard Copeland for his insights into Yootha, and the invaluable help I got from Tony Lee at www.bigredbook.com.info/ . I'm very grateful to Paul O'Grady, and his producer Michael Prince, for giving my book the honour of a mention on *The Paul O'Grady Show* on BBC Radio 2.

Credits

The Yootha Joyce Archive, Glynn Edwards, Michele Briant at *TV Times*, Alistair Smith at *The Stage*, Jeff Vickers MBE, Bert Hill, Viv Jones and the late Tom (Hardy) Jones, Karen Fisher, Murray Melvin, at Theatre Royal Stratford East for the use of images, also Peter Roos and Brian Cooke. Every effort was made to trace those holding additional copyright material, and to those I omitted, I would happily add appropriate credit in any further editions of this book.

Introduction

Writing *Dear Yootha… The Life of Yootha Joyce*, which I finally completed last year, was one of the happiest periods of my life. It made me realise just how kind people were to offer help completing what was quite a difficult task. Aware of the need to keep Yootha's biography focused and tight, I was forced to leave a lot of information about her out of the finished manuscript, which I didn't want to be patchy or disjointed. So much material was left out, in fact, that I began to see that it would make another, rather different, book – a kind of companion to the biography.

The research I have completed over the years about Yootha's life and career has always been a pleasure to do. I still get a buzz of excitement whenever I uncover anything related to her. I am sure that at the beginning of her career she cultivated the style that transfixed many people who worked, loved, knew and watched her. Since finishing the biography, a fair amount of additional material has surfaced, too: the interview with Terence Lee Dickson was perhaps the most valuable new contribution. In his review of *Dear Yootha…*, Greg Jameson at entertainment-focus.com/, describes Yootha as an "enigma": and so she was – as we know, she would barely talk about herself. But new information helps us get that little bit closer.

I have come to realise how Yootha in the end felt that her career was a failure. This stemmed, it seems, from early childhood insecurities which are alluded to in this scrapbook. Had she been alive, she would now (in 2015) be 88. I often wonder where she would have been in the business today, had she been alive.

In what follows, wherever possible I have used quotations from people, many of whom I interviewed, to give the book continuity. Where this was not possible, I have used quotations from *Dear Yootha…* to build up the story and add vital details.

Much of the information I have about Yootha's background and childhood comes from a photograph album and small scrapbook that her mother, Maud kept from September 1910 onwards. It contains contributions, in the form of poems, songs, drawings and cuttings, from her friends and family. The opening page gives some idea of its contents:

> You may look at this album
> But learn ere you look,
> That all are requested to add to this book.
>
> You may quiz as you please,
> But the penalty is:-
> That you likewise leave something
> For others to quiz.
>
> Owner.
> Sept. 19th. 1910.

I urge you, dear reader, to follow Maud's instructions; and, if you possibly can, add to and research further, any information on Yootha's life and career, when time allows you.

PAUL CURRAN, 20TH AUGUST 2015.

The Yootha Joyce Scrapbook.

"All my family sang: they were all musically talented, and would play musical instruments." YOOTHA JOYCE

Yootha's Grandparents, William and Jessica Rebecca (Left & Right)
Yootha's Mum and Dad, Hurst and Jessica Maud, on the rocks in Devon 1925

"They had nothing one minute, then everything to eat and wear the next" YOOTHA JOYCE

> "Maud is going to sing a song
> "But me in my little Bed."
> I should have accompanied her,
> But unfortunatley I have a poisoned head"
> Yootha's Dad and Uncle write about Yootha's Mum.

"Mother went walking on Wandsworth Common after feeling stuffy watching Hurst at the Clapham Grand Theatre."
YOOTHA, ON THE DAY OF HER BIRTH

(From Our Own Correspondent.)
PRINCES (M.D., Francis Latimer; M. Frank Yearsley; Mus.D., Fred Elkin).— "The Padre," which is being presented here this week, is a happy play on the light side in which Braughy Williams plays the title-rôle. The padre in question has learned something of the world by his experiences of the war, and into the little French village of which he is cure there comes a war profiteer and his wife, who was once a revue star. It is around these three that the story revolves, and a very interesting story it proves. Albert Darnley acts the part of the profiteer, and Minnie Love is a capital comedienne in the role of the wife. Raymond Langley as Pierre de Sableuse makes a good impression, and others in the cast who do well are Betty Rubens as Estelle and Cyril Jervis (Walter).

The billing from The Clapham Grand Theatre the day of Yootha's birth. with no mention at all of Hurst.

YOOTHA ROSE and HARRY J. ROWLAND
Offer
ENTER
ECSTASY!!
The "More than a" Concert Party.
SUMMER TOUR COMPLETE.
VACANT
APRIL 23, MAY 7, OCTOBER 15 on
ROSE & ROWLAND, 15, Pond Place, S.W.3.

Yootha Rose, the performer that Yootha claimed she was named after.

Hurst and Maud had been married for some two years when Yootha, their only child, was born, on 20th August 1927. It's a curious name, by any stretch of the imagination; Yootha later admitted she 'loathed and detested it.' Yootha Rose, the famous singer, toy maker and trustee for the National Toy Museum, began to sing during the war, at concert parties in the UK. Her father, the Australian singer Charles Rose, had toured with Nellie Melba, one of the most famous singers of her time. According again to Yootha, at the time of her birth, Yootha Rose would be performing at the same time as Hurst was, but again, the cast lists from her tours do not feature him. In an interview for the book This is Their Lives *by Jonathan Meades in 1980, Yootha claimed that Yootha Rose was 'a dancer on the same bill in Clapham as her father.' she said, "She owes her name to her mother's indecision. She had no idea what to call the child, so the baby's grandmother suggested that she be called after the next woman to walk through the door of the nursing home ward. This turned out to be Yootha Rose.* **DEAR YOOTHA…THE LIFE OF YOOTHA JOYCE**

Yootha's birth registration, 1927, and as a baby. (Right)

"Yootha's parents were convinced they were having a boy. When a girl arrived, they were in shock. Hence the business about the name. They had nothing planned for a girl." **CHRISTINE PILGRIM**

Yootha on Brighton beach, 1929

"My nose was as wide as my mouth. It actually touched my left ear. That straightened out, but the mouth didn't."
YOOTHA JOYCE

"My parents were away so much - I'm sure [Hurst] would have done a moonlight flit if he could. And so would I - but my mother would sooner have pawned me" **YOOTHA JOYCE**

Battersea Co - Ed School, which Yootha called a "Marvellous place".

"Yootha hasn't quite the tone her mother has" HURST NEEDHAM

"My aunts and father thought I couldn't play the piano or sing like them: in fact, they didn't think I was much good at anything. - When you're eleven or twelve that destroys you. I wasn't desperately fond of him"" YOOTHA JOYCE

One can imagine that these comments must have angered and upset her: the main impression, however, is that Yootha had a permanent sense of her own inadequacy, and that this, in turn, made her anxious to prove herself. She felt determined to prove her parents wrong, to excel at something, anything, rather than be "not quite as good as the family." At this point in her life, she said, she had "the fighting instinct to the fore. DEAR YOOTHA…THE LIFE OF YOOTHA JOYCE

Yootha declared she was to be an actress; no one could understand why she had chosen such a profession. Maybe her experience with the touring theatre company, or the drama experiences when she was evacuated at Petersfield had given her some inspiration? Yootha later claimed that her decision to become an actress was based on the fact that "nobody knew what to do with me." DEAR YOOTHA…THE LIFE OF YOOTHA JOYCE

```
                    ROYAL ACADEMY OF DRAMATIC ART.
                    MIDDLE A.  TIMETABLE. SPRING 1945.

                                              MISS CARRINGTON    R.7
MONDAY.    10.0-12.0    Acting
           12.0-1.0     LUNCH                 MISS WARREN        R.3
           1.0-2.0      V.P.G.                MR. JEYNES         R.9
           1.30-2.0     Diction M.            MR. FROESCHLEN     R.1
           2.0-3.0      Fencing               MISS BOWIE         R.5
           3.0-4.0      Diction G.            MR. CONSTABLE      R.R.
Sp.C.      4.15-5.15    Youth Movement        MR. CONSTABLE      R.R.
           5.15-5.45    Remedial Movement     MISS WARREN        R.3
           4.15-5.15    Remedial V.P.G.                          R.6
           4.15-5.15    P.R. if needed
                                              MR. RANALOW        R.4
TUESDAY.   10.30-11.0   V.P.M.                                   R.6
           11.0-12.0    P.R.                  MISS PHILLIPS      R.1
           12.0-1.0     Acting
           1.0-2.0      LUNCH                                    R.6
           2.0-3.0      P.R.                  MR. CONSTABLE      R.R.
           3.0-4.0      Basic Movement        MR. CONSTABLE      R.2
Sp.C.      4.15-5.15    Youth Movement        MISS DAVIS         R.4
           4.          Special Verse                             R.6
           4.15-5.15    P.R. if needed
                                              MISS PHILLIPS      R.R.
WEDNESDAY. 10.0-11.0    Mime                  MISS CARRINGTON    R.1
           11.0-12.0    Acting
           1.0-2.0      LUNCH                 MISS WARREN        R.3
           2.0-3.0      V.P.G.                MR. JEYNES         R.9
           2.0-2.30     Diction M.                               R.6
           3.0-4.0      P.R.                  MISS WARREN        R.3
Sp.C.      4.15-5.15    Remedial V.P.G.
                                              MR. RANALOW        R.4
THURSDAY.  10.0-10.30   V.P.M.                MISS BOWIE         R.5
           11.0-12.0    Diction G.            MISS FLETCHER      R.R
           12.0-1.0     Dancing
           1.0-2.0      LUNCH                 MISS PHILLIPS      T.
           2.0-5.0      Acting
                                              DAME IRENE VANBURGH
FRIDAY.    10.0-11.0    Talk                  MISS PHILLIPS      R.
           11.0-1.0     Acting
           1.0-2.0      LUNCH                 MISS PHILLIPS      R.
           2.0-3.0      Mime                  MISS DAVIS         R.
           3.0-4.0      Verse                                    R.
           4.15-5.15    Principal's Lecture   MISS BEDELLS       Studio
Sp.C.      5.30-6.30    Special Dancing
```

A weeks schedule for Yootha, studying at RADA 1944.

Work & Performance Highlights 1945

Pride and Prejudice. (THEATRE)
By Jane Austen
Role - Lydia Bennet

Henry V. (THEATRE)
By William Shakespeare
Role 1.- Archbishop of Canterbury
Role 2.- Private John Bates

"Yootha, like the other girls, would often have to take on the male roles. - She was always ready for a laugh, as was Lois (Maxwell), when we performed together." ROGER MOORE

This Happy Breed. (THEATRE)
By Noel Coward
Role - Sylvia

ROYAL ACADEMY OF DRAMATIC ART

Performance by U.M.2a

Thursday 12th July 1945 at 2.30 p.m.
&
Friday 13th July 1945 at 2.0 p.m

"THIS HAPPY BREED"
by
Noel Coward

PRODUCED BY RONALD KERR   LIGHTING BY COLIN CHANDLER

Characters in Order of Appearance:

Mrs. Flint.................Robin Cockburn
                          Sonia Cayley
Ethel.....................Pamela Pitchford
                          Jane Cotton
                          Jose Lloyd Thomas
                          Pamela Pitchford
Sylvia....................Yootha Joyce
                          Mary Clayton
                          Christine Gant
                          Elizabeth Lefebure
Frank Gibbons.............William Walker
Bob Mitchell..............Roger Moore
Reg.......................Ian Whittaker (U.M.2.b)
                          John Scott

"A sense of comedy – Good" RADA notes from '**This Happy Breed**' 1945.

Escape Me Never. (THEATRE)
By Margaret Kennedy
Role – Girl

It is very noticeable in this production, that the small-part actors have taken great pains. Jack Martyn, as a butler, and Walter Plinge, Yootha Joyce and John Thomas in the coffee stall scene, are worth special attention.

Yootha's first review for '**Escape Me Never**' 1945.

Yootha was certainly restless and eager to perform: she remembered walking down Croydon High Street with her mother one day, and popping into the Grand to ask for an acting job. The Arthur Lane repertory company, who were based at the theatre, laughed at Yootha's request, saying "yeah, like you and 5,000 other people".
Yootha's first role was in the Margaret Kennedy play **Escape Me Never**, *a sequel to* **The Constant Nymph**, *beginning on 23rd July 1945.*
The Croydon Advertiser *on 27th July 1945 comments: "The ingenuity shown by the minor characters make this play not to be missed"* **DEAR YOOTHA… THE LIFE OF YOOTHA JOYCE**

Autumn Crocus. (THEATRE)
By Dodie Smith
Role - The Young Lady Living in Sin, (also credited as A.S.M.)

In Dodie Smith's **Autumn Crocus**. *Yootha was 'The Young Lady Living in Sin': a type of character role that would follow her around in the years ahead.*
"If her current performance is any criterion, Yootha Joyce is a young lady of whom we may expect great things. Let us hope that the producer will show equal discrimination in casting her for future presentations." The review [in **The Croydon Advertiser**] *also picks up on a mistake in the sound effects that might have been Yootha's fault. It remarks on the "blows of a hooter on the O.P side, when the bus is supposed to drive up on the prompt side?"*
Yootha remembered her work as an assistant stage manager as tough going: "in those days five sets had to be changed in 30 seconds, and if you missed a single fork in the restaurant scene, you were had up." Once, she recalled she had to "hold up a fireplace for an act while the stagehands cursed and bashed behind her off-stage." **DEAR YOOTHA… THE LIFE OF YOOTHA JOYCE**

Cymbeline. (THEATRE)
By William Shakespeare
Role 1 - Lord
Role 2 - Imogen

Heartbreak House . (THEATRE)
By George Bernard Shaw
Role - Lady Utterwood

"The head said I was no good, but he usually said that about everybody, - all the awards went to Juliets and Desdemonas, and I'm a bit strong for them." **YOOTHA JOYCE ON HER LAST TERM AT RADA**

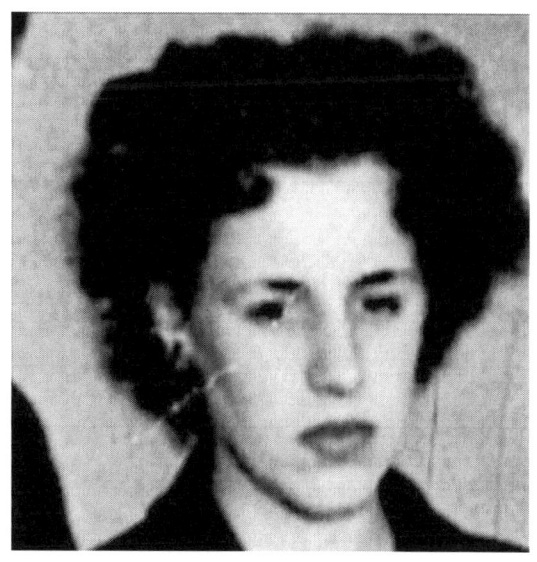

Work & Performance Highlights 1946

You Cant Take It With You. (THEATRE)
By Moss Hart & George Kaufman.
Role - Essie

```
ROYAL ACADEMY OF DRAMATIC ART
        Performance by U.M.1b
   Monday, 18th February 1946 at 2.30 pm
       "YOU CAN'T TAKE IT WITH YOU"
                  by
         Moss Hart & George S. Kaufman
           PRODUCED BY HUGH MILLER

Penelope Sycamore........  Elizabeth Digby-Smith  too fussy
                           Bette Bollard         improved consonants
                           Audrey Myhill         competent

Essie.....................  Joyce Elphick        good
                           Caroline Penney       attractive
                           Yootha Joyce          unattractive

Rheba....................  Jacqueline Boiteux   don't drop voice
```

> RADA notes from **'You Can't Take It With You'**, 1946. "Unattractive"!

She Stoops To Conquer. (THEATRE)
By Oliver Goldsmith
Role - Kate Hardcastle

"They all thought I was the worst actress they ever had in the whole of their history, and I'd need a further two years before I could make a living, so I left. - It was not really my cup of tea," YOOTHA JOYCE

```
UPPER MIDDLE 1B.

JEAN ANDERSON.          3.   1 PD
SHIRLEY BAGRITT.        4.   UM
DACIA BATTYE.           5.   Not allowed to return
PATRICIA BERRY.         5.   Not moved up.
BRENDA COOPER.          3.   Leverhulme Exhibition 1 PD
DELIA DIGBY.            4.   Left
HEATHER FREEDLAND.      3.   Leverhulme Exhibition 1 PD
CHRISTINE GANT.         4.   UM
SYLVIA GLOVER-CLARK.    4.   27
DAPHNE HARVEY.          4.   Advise doubtful
YOOTHA JOYCE.           4.   UM - bad attendance.
ADELE LEIGH.            3.   UM
```

> "Bad attendance" at RADA.

Butlins Holiday Camp Theatre (Skegness) *With The Forbes Russell Players [The London Company.]
They Walk Alone. (THEATRE)
By Max Catto
Role – Emmy Baudine
9-27/08/1946

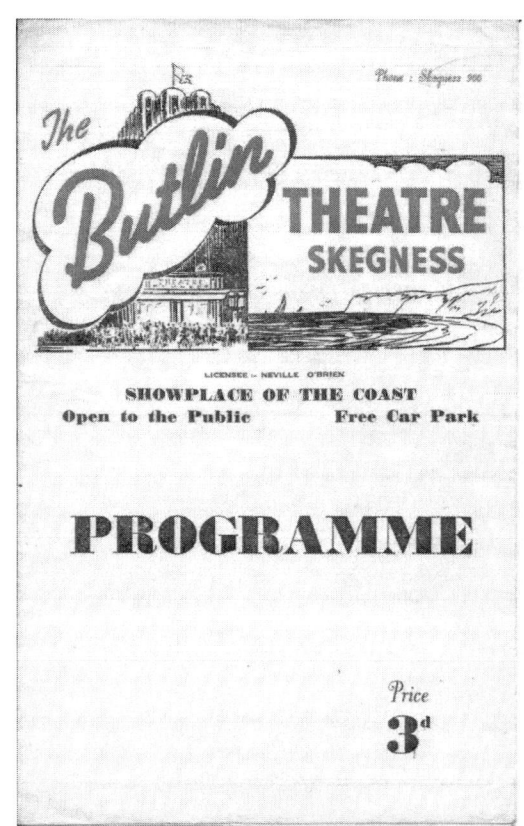

PROGRAMME.

Forbes Russell
Presents
HIS LONDON COMPANY in
"THEY WALK ALONE"
By
MAX CATTO

Cast in order of appearance:—

Julie Tallent	...	Jacqueline Desmond
Bess Stanforth	...	Marjorie Mee Jones.
Mr. Tallent	...	Sidney Trevelyan
Robert Stanforth	...	Peter Allenby.
Larry Tallent	...	John Seebold.
Emmy Baudine	...	Youtha Joyce
Saul Trevithick	...	Douglas Morison.

The Play Directed By
John Seebold.

The action of the play takes place in the living-room of the Tallents' farm, near Lincoln.

Synopsis of Scenes:—

Act I.
Scene I.   Early Evening
Scene II.   An afternoon three weeks later

Act II.
Scene I.   Evening four weeks later
Scene II.   After midnight, four hours later
Scene III.   An hour and a half later

Act III.
About three hours later, approaching dawn.

Scenery Painted and Designed by
D. Donnelly Barker.

Lighting By   Strand Elect & Eng. Co. Ltd.,
Furniture By   A. & J. Best, Boston.
Telephone Kindly Loaned By   The G.P.O.

General Manager   JOHN SEEBOLD.
Stage Manager   For Forbes Russell   ROBERT DUNCAN.
Assistant Stage Manager   JOYCE ELPHIC.

While The Sun Shines.
Role – Unknown
9-27/08/1946

Interior of Butlins 'Gaiety' Theatre, Skegness 1946.

Work & Performance Highlights 1947

ENSA tours, (No Records)
The Merchant of Venice. (THEATRE)
By William Shakespeare
Role - Portia? (Unknown)

*"Apparently, I wasn't a bad Portia,- but I always thought she was a drip.- In my repertory days, there was 'a Shakespeare voice' and a 'Shakespeare attitude'. Everyone was trying that, and all sorts of Christopher Fry things.-
I consider my work to be the most important thing," as she said. Yootha had the capacity to play a wide variety of parts, and enjoyed contrasts and challenges. She said she found "top people so boring in the classical theatre," DEAR YOOTHA… THE LIFE OF YOOTHA JOYCE*

Work & Performance Highlights 1948

Humoresque. (THEATRE) [The Harry Kendall Players]
By Fanny Hurst
Role - Peony Barker

"HUMORESQUE"

On Tuesday was presented here a play in three acts and six scenes, by Guy Bolton, entitled "Humoresque."

Described by the author as a comedy of youth, this very modern little piece proves itself to be a light, breezy, and wittily written after-dinner play in the familiar surroundings of students' apartments. In this case the young people are students of music, and we find them in the rooms shared by Bob, a gay young man, and Richard, his serious-minded companion. On the arrival on the scene of Kay, a charming student of the pianoforte, they both fall in love with her. After a few minor quarrels she promises herself to Richard. There is very little story to worry about; but this does not matter very much, because the dialogue is so crisp.

Harry Kendall, who has produced the play, sets a cracking pace and sees to it that it does not slacken. The young cast enter into the tempo with good spirit. Although, apart from the two leading male parts, there is little chance of characterisation, they all work to make a success. As Bob, the flippant half-section of the tenants' apartment, Charles Grainger is a host in himself. Admitted he is given most of the "plum" lines, but he makes admirable use of them, and his animated method of delivery and sprightly action prove very acceptable. As his serious-minded colleague, Richard, Grey Blake sets a fine contrast. His playing of the part has the effect of gently sobering up the frivolous element without applying the brake too much. Ursula Howells is a charming and quite sincere Kay, who hits the right mood with each of the two young men. Yootha Joyce is successful as a boisterous young lady student, and Harold Scott makes a dignified but warm-hearted professor of music. Johnnie Schofield has some amusing moments as Daly, the Irish factotum. Alun Owen and Richard Curnock add their quotas as two students.

Farewell Earth's Bliss (RADIO)
(A portrait of the 1665 Plague of London. Compiled and written from contemporary sources by Terence Tiller)
BBC Third Programme
Role- Third woman
01/12/48

Work & Performance Highlights 1949

Hay Fever. (THEATRE)
By Noel Coward
Role – Unknown

Hippodrome. — Reginald Salberg's Players are directed by John Maxwell, in "Hay Fever," with Peggy Mount giving a droll performance as Judith Bliss. Anthony Finigan (Simon) and Pamela Tiffen (Sorel) participate with distinction in the almost continuous hilarity. Adequate support is given by Doreen Andrew, Tim Hudson, Derek Benfield, Yootha Joyce, David Garth, and Jean Burgess.

Work & Performance Highlights 1951

THEATRE ROYAL
ASHTON-UNDER-LYNE

THE JACK ROSE
REPERTORY PLAYERS
PROGRAMME — PRICE 2d.

ASHTON-UNDER-LYNE

The Jack Rose Players continued their successful season here with "Mother of Men." Among the plays presented during the past four months have been "Nothing but the Truth," "The Light of Heart," "Mountain Air," "Night Must Fall," "The Perfect Woman," "Grand National Night," and "A Lady Mislaid." The company comprises Kenneth Keeling, Heather Chasen, Derek Benfield, Yootha Joyce, John Chilvers, Ursula Camm, Roy Deeley, Enid McCall, Patricia Wilmore, Gordon Rollings, Kathleen Deva, Miles Glaister, Frank Lloyd, Patrick Johns, and Belle Brierley. The plays have been produced by Kenneth Keeling and Derek Benfield.

"Monday-Friday once nightly at 7.45 - Two houses on Saturday 6.15 and 8.30"

Peace Comes to Peckham. (THEATRE)
By R.F Delderfield
Role – Grace

Nothing But The Truth. (THEATRE)
By James Montgomery
Role – Unknown

The Light of Heart. (THEATRE)
By Emlyn Williams
Role – Unknown

The Ten-Five Never Stops (THEATRE)
By John Essex
Role – Trixy Evans

THEATRE ROYAL
ASHTON-UNDER-LYNE
Telephone 1252 — Manager: Jack Wood

MONDAY, APRIL 30th, 1951 — FOR ONE WEEK — ONCE NIGHTLY at 7-30 — SATURDAY at 6-15 and 8-30

CONTACT THEATRICAL PRODUCTIONS LIMITED PRESENT

THE JACK ROSE REPERTORY PLAYERS
in
"THE TEN-FIVE NEVER STOPS"
By JOHN ESSEX

Cast in order of appearance:

Sally Baines	HEATHER CHASEN
Andrew Baines	JOHN CHILVERS
Trixy Evans	YOOTHA JOYCE
Jim Vatcher	KENNETH KEELING
Philip Ryder	ROY DEELEY
Dan Evans	DEREK BENFIELD
Dr. Harrington	MILES GLAISTER
Inspector Warren	PATRICK JOHNS

Play Produced by KENNETH KEELING
Setting Designed and Painted by INIGO MONK
The Production Directed by JACK ROSE

Stage Director .... MILES GLAISTER
Stage Managers .... PATRICIA WILMOUR and PATRICK JOHNS

SYNOPSIS OF SCENES

The Scene of the Play is laid in the Station-Master's house adjoining Gallowsclough Junction.
TIME—1948

ACT I .... Saturday Night
— INTERVAL TEN MINUTES —
ACT II .... Wednesday Morning
— INTERVAL TEN MINUTES —
ACT III .... Wednesday Night

Scenery and Properties built and made in our own workshops. Special lighting and effects by Strand Electric Engineering Co. Telephone by courtesy of G.P.O. Radio by Chisnall, Warrington St., Ashton. China, Glassware and Ornaments, etc., by the Pottery Gift Shop, 140 Stamford St. Silver and Plate, etc., Kenworthy, Stamford St. Special Ladies Hairdressing, Deborrah, 70 Katherine St. Flowers by Cox of Old St. Fireplaces and Household Goods by J. W. Hall, The Grate House. Furniture by Haughs, Oldham Rd., and Harrison's Old St. Furs by Stansfields, Old St., Ashton. Leather Goods by Bowers, Stamford St. Gramophone Records supplied by Rex Hoult, Stamford St. Nylon Stockings by Kayser-Bondor. Cigarettes by Abdulla.

ERIC LEWIS—at the Piano

Mountain Air. (THEATRE)
Author Unknown
Role – Unknown

Night Must Fall. (THEATRE)
By Emlyn Williams
Role – Unknown

Grand National Night. (THEATRE)
By Campell & Dorothy Christie
Role – Babs

"GRAND NATIONAL NIGHT"
By DOROTHY and CAMPBELL CHRISTIE

Gerald Coates, a wealthy shipowner living near Liverpool, has a drunken and worthless wife, Babs. She was a barmaid and married Gerald when he was only a clerk. On Grand National night Gerald is alone at home. Babs returns from Aintree intoxicated. It is known that she has been associating with a dissolute racing man in Liverpool. During a quarrel she attacks Gerald with a knife and she is accidentally killed. Gerald decides, impulsively, to hide the body, fearing that he may not be able to prove his innocence. The next day Babs' sister Pinkie arrives, disturbed because Babs is not where she was expected to be. Then Babs' body is found some miles from Liverpool. The police investigate and several unfortunate circumstances are revealed. The net slowly closes and Gerald is eventually in imminent danger of arrest, having compromised himself badly.

The play has an unusual and satisfying finish. This is real good theatre.

Dear Patrons,

It is evident by the remarks I have heard in the Theatre this week that you are keenly interested in the players, and it is my intention to let you know something about them all. This week I give you a pen portrait of Miss Heather Chasen.

Heather Chasen was born in Singapore. At the age of fourteen she escaped just before it fell to the Japanese.

Having studied at the Royal Academy of Dramatic Art, went into Repertory and has done several tours. She played the leading part in the film "Meet the Duke", in which she scored an instant success. Because of this she was cast for a part in "The Wicked Lady" with Margaret Lockwood. She much prefers the more interesting work of the theatre and is looking forward to a continued stay in Ashton, where there are some excellent leading roles lined up for her.

Her main hobby is the care of her miniature Dachshund, who is as much at home in the theatre as her mistress.

Yours sincerely,
JACK ROSE.

A Lady Mislaid. (THEATRE)
By Kenneth Horne [the playwright, not the comedian]
Role – Unknown

PROGRAMME

Monday to Friday Once Nightly at 7.45 — Saturday Two Houses at 6.15 and 8.30

CONTACT THEATRICAL PRODUCTIONS LTD. present

THE JACK ROSE REPERTORY PLAYERS
IN
"A LADY MISLAID"
By KENNETH HORNE

CAST IN ORDER OF APPEARANCE

Mrs. Small (Daily Woman) ... Ursula Camm
Jennifer (Younger Sister) ... Heather Chasen
Esther (Elder Sister) .... Yootha Joyce
Bullock (Detective) .... Derek Benfield
Visitor .... John Chilvers
George (Jennifer's Fiance) ... Patrick Johns
Young Woman .... Patricia Wilmour

SCENES: The living room at "Manor Cottage," the home of Esther and Jennifer Williams.

Act I. Scene 1. Early morning.
Scene 2. That evening.

10 MINUTES INTERVAL

Act II. Scene 1. Some hours later.
Scene 2. Early the next morning.

10 MINUTES INTERVAL

Act III. Later that morning.

The Perfect Woman. (THEATRE)
By Wallace Geoffrey
Role – Esther

"There was one incident when I was meant to descend a huge staircase looking very glamorous. I was the ugly duckling turned into the beautiful swan, and as I was holding on to my leading man, my knicker elastic broke, and they slid down my thigh. I was walking crossed legged trying to keep them up, and as I got down to the bottom of the stairs they fell round my ankles, so I just bent down and picked them up, rolled them up and put them in my leading man's pocket. I don't think anybody noticed. Then we walked around and he said, 'what was that you put in my pocket Yootha?' 'My knickers luv' was my reply." YOOTHA JOYCE

The Seventh Veil. (THEATRE)
By S & M Box
Role – Unknown

"I left the piano to rush into my sweetheart's arms, and the piano went on playing." YOOTHA JOYCE

Mother Of Men. (THEATRE)
By Ada G. Abbott
Role – Unknown

"I went to a matinee to see the film All About Eve *with Bette Davis"* (which is supposed to be based on the life of Tallulah Bankhead, whom Yootha would later work with). She usually had Thursday afternoons off: *"we would usually work in the morning and evening, however, sitting there I overheard two ladies behind me saying how lovely it was to have Thursday afternoon off to go to the pictures. It was three in the afternoon and I was supposed to be on at 2.30! I completely missed my performance. That was the only time in my life I'd missed one, and I sweated blood. I should have been fired but they didn't do that, they were very sweet about it."* DEAR YOOTHA… THE LIFE OF YOOTHA JOYCE

The Paragon (THEATRE)
By Roland and Michael Pertwee
Role - Joan

PROGRAMME

Monday to Friday Once Nightly at 7.45 — Saturday Two Houses at 6.15 and 8.30

CONTACT THEATRICAL PRODUCTIONS LTD. present

THE JACK ROSE REPERTORY PLAYERS

IN

"THE PARAGON"

BY ROLAND AND MICHAEL PERTWEE

CAST IN ORDER OF APPEARANCE

Delivery Man	Miles Glaister
Kate	Margaret Evans
Joan	Yootha Joyce
Jessica	Ursula Camm
The Earl of Clandon	John Chilvers
Sir Robert Rawley	Kenneth Keeling
Angela	Patricia Wilmour
Maxwell Oliver	Patrick Johns
The Unknown Man	Edward Leslie

Play Produced by KENNETH KEELING
Setting Designed and Painted by JIM MacINTYRE
The Production Directed by JACK ROSE

Stage Director .... MILES GLAISTER
Stage Manager .... PATRICIA WILMOUR
Assistant Stage Manager ..... MARGARET EVANS

SCENE ... Sir Robert Rawley's House in the Vale of Avalon.

ACT 1 ... Scene 1. A spring afternoon.
Scene 2. An hour later.

15 Minutes Interval

ACT 2 ... The Action is continuous.
Time — 1946.

Scenery and Properties built and made in our own workshops. Special lighting and effects by Strand Electric Engineering Co. Telephone by courtesy of G.P.O. Radio by Chisnall, Warrington St., Ashton. China, Glassware and Ornaments, etc., by the Pottery Gift Shop, 140 Stamford St. Silver and Plate, etc., Kenworthy, Stamford St. Special Ladies' Hairdressing, Deborrah, 70 Katherine St. Flowers by Cox of Old St. Fireplaces and Household Goods by J. W. Hall. The Grate House. Furniture by Hough's, Oldham Rd. Furs by Stansfield, Old St. Leather Goods by Bowers, Stamford St. Gramophone Records supplied by Rex Hoult, Stamford St. Stationery: Burgess & Dyson, The Avenue, Ashton. Ladies' hats and handbags: Hollywood Hats, Stamford St., Ashton. Nylon Stockings by Kayser-Bondor. Cigarettes by Abdulla.

THE ROTTERS

BY H. F. MALTBY

"The Rotters" is not, as the title might suggest, a drama about low types in Soho, but is one of the funniest Lancashire comedies ever written. A straight-laced self-made Lancashire business man rules his family with a heavy rod of respectability and frowns upon the slightest straying from the straight and narrow. One by one his family slip, the impish youngest daughter runs away from school, the eldest daughter acts indiscreetly with the Public School chauffeur, and the son ... but come along and see for yourselves how the story builds up to a truly hilarious climax.

H. F. Maltby is a guarantee of high class entertainment and has been for many years, "The Rotters" is undoubtedly his finest comedy. You will enjoy an evening full of laughter and fun with "The Rotters."

The Rotters (THEATRE)
By H F Maltby
Role - Unknown

SIDES (BROOKSIDE BREWERY)

ASHTON-UNDER-LYNE

BOTTLERS OF GUINNESS "HARP LABEL" STOUT

SUPPLIED IN THE THEATRE BAR

PROGRAMME

Monday to Friday Once Nightly at 7.45 — Saturday Two Houses at 6.15 and 8.30

CONTACT THEATRICAL PRODUCTIONS LTD. present

THE JACK ROSE REPERTORY PLAYERS

IN

"CHARLEY'S AUNT"

By BRADON THOMAS

CAST IN ORDER OF APPEARANCE

Jack Chesney	PHILIP NEWMAN
Brassett	KENNETH KEELING
Charley Wykeham	DONALD McKILLOP
Lord Fancourt Babberly	LEONARD LEWIS
Kitty	JOANNA GLASS
Amy	YOOTHA JOYCE
Sir Francis Chesney	JOHN CHILVERS
Stephen Spettigue	ROBIN WENTWORTH
Donna Lucia D'Alvadorez	URSULA CAMM
Ela Delahay	PATRICIA WILMOUR

Play Produced by KENNETH KEELING
Settings painted by JIM GODFREY
The Production Directed by JACK ROSE

Stage Director .... LEONARD LEWIS
Stage Manager .... DONALD McKILLOP

SCENES

ACT I. Jack Chesney's Room in College
—Morning.

10 Minutes Interval

ACT II. Garden outside Jack Chesney's Rooms.
—Afternoon.

10 Minutes Interval

ACT III. Drawing room at Spettigue's House.
Evening.

ACKNOWLEDGMENTS

All Modern Furnishings by The Cash Furnishing Company

Scenery and Properties built and made in our own workshops. Special lighting and effects by Strand Electric Engineering Co. Telephone by courtesy of G.P.O. China, Glassware and Ornaments etc. by the Pottery Gift Shop, Stamford Street. Brassware by Hill & Bottomley, Stamford Street. Silver and Plate by Kenworthy, Stamford Street. Furs by Stansfield, Old Street. Gramophone Records. Electric Clocks and Radios by Rex Hoult, Stamford Street. Stationery by Burgess and Dyson, The Avenue, Ladies' hats and handbags by Hollywood Hats, Stamford Street. Nylon Stockings by Kayser-Bondor. Smokers requisites by G. S. Shaw, Bow Street, Ashton. Cigarettes by Abdulla.

THE GHOST TRAIN

By ARNOLD RIDLEY

The pulling of a communication cord by a very silly young man is responsible for six weary passengers missing their connection for Truro, and finding themselves stranded on a stormy night at a small wayside station in Cornwall. Against the advice of a queer psychic stationmaster, who tells them weird stories of a ghost train, they decide to stay the night in the waiting-room with the intention of catching the first train on in the morning. Before long they are regretting this decision. First of all the stationmaster is found dead outside the door, then a young lady in evening dress puts in an appearance followed by her brother and a so-called doctor. This lady also being psychic is supposed to be attracted to the station whenever the ghost train is due, and when in the middle of the night this apparition rushes through, she becomes hysterical. This is followed by a visit of ghostly forms, one of which is shot by the silly young man, and turns out to be the brother of the lady in evening dress. From now on the young man takes command and exposes these late arrivals.

This is a brilliant play, full of comedy, thrills and drama.

Charley's Aunt (THEATRE)
By Bradon Thomas
Role – Amy

The Ghost Train (THEATRE)
By Arnold Ridley
Role - Unknown

The Devil a Saint (THEATRE)
By Lesley Storm
Role – Sarah Jane

PROGRAMME

Monday to Friday Once Nightly at 7.45 — Saturday Two Houses at 6.15 and 8.30

CONTACT THEATRICAL PRODUCTIONS LTD. present

THE JACK ROSE REPERTORY PLAYERS
IN
"THE DEVIL A SAINT"
by LESLEY STORM

CAST IN ORDER OF APPEARANCE

Sarah Jane	Yootha Joyce
Josiah Skinthorne	Kenneth Keeling
Seth Farrar	Robin Wentworth
Betty Skinthorne	Patricia Wilmour
Dr. Dennis Metcalfe	Patrick Johns
Mrs. Threappleton	Ursula Camm
The Rev. Mr. Cummings	John Chilvers

SCENE—The Action of the play takes place in the Sitting Room-Business-Office of Mr. Josiah Skinthorne's House somewhere in the North Midlands.

ACT 1—About 11-30 a.m. one morning.
10 Minutes Interval
ACT 2—The Action is continuous.
10 Minutes Interval
ACT 3—The Action is again continuous.

Black Chiffon (THEATRE)
By Lesley Storm
Role - Unknown

Bed of Roses (THEATRE)
By Falkland L Cary
Role - Jenny Pickersgill

THEATRE ROYAL
Telephone 1262 — ASHTON-UNDER-LYNE — Manager: Jack Wood

MONDAY, 26th MARCH, 1951 — FOR ONE WEEK — ONCE NIGHTLY at 7-30 — SATURDAY at 6-15 and 8-30

CONTACT THEATRICAL PRODUCTIONS LIMITED PRESENT

THE JACK ROSE REPERTORY PLAYERS
IN
"BED OF ROSES"
By FALKLAND L. CARY

Cast in order of appearance:

Jenny Pickersgill	YOOTHA JOYCE
Pam Pickersgill	PATRICIA WILMOUR
Mrs. Blisten	URSULA CAMM
Bob Huggins	DEREK BENFIELD
Rose Pickersgill	HEATHER CHASEN
Mat Pickersgill	KENNETH KEELING
Basil Graves	JOHN CHILVERS
Dr. Raheny	MORRIS PARSONS
May Rossiter	PAT STEVENSON

SCENE: The action of the play passes in the Living Room of the Pickersgill house in Corporation Street, Hinton.

TIME—THE PRESENT

ACT I — Late Afternoon
INTERVAL TEN MINUTES
ACT II — Afternoon. A Week Later
INTERVAL TEN MINUTES
ACT III — Late Afternoon. Two Days Later

Scenery and Properties built and made in our own workshops. Special lighting and effects by Strand Electric Engineering Co. Telephones by courtesy of G.P.O. Radio by Chisnall, Warrington St. Ashton. China, Glassware and Ornaments, etc., by the Pottery Gift Shop, 140 Stamford St. Silver and Plate, etc., Kenworthy, Stamford St. Special Ladies Hairdressing, Deborah, 70 Katherine St. Flowers by Cox of Old St. Fireplace and Household Goods by J. W. Hall, The Gem House, Furniture by Hough's Oldham Rd. Leather Goods by Bowers, Stamford St. Nylon Stockings by Kayser-Bondor. Cigarettes by Abdulla.

ERIC LEWIS—at the Piano
Overture—"MINUET IN G" ... By Paderewski
Interval—"MELODY IN F" ... Rubinstein
Interval—"NOCTURNE IN E FLAT" ... Chopin

Play Produced by KENNETH KEELING
Setting Designed and Painted by INIGO MONK
The Production Directed by JACK ROSE

Stage Director ... MILES GLAISTER
Stage Manager ... PATRICIA WILMOUR
Assistant Stage Manager ... DAVID BOLIVER

While Parents Sleep (THEATRE)
By Anthony Kimmins
Role - Nanny

But Once a Year (THEATRE)
By Falkland L. Cary
Role - Olivia Meldon

PROGRAMME

Monday to Friday Once Nightly at 7.45 — Saturday Two Houses at 6.15 and 8.30

CONTACT THEATRICAL PRODUCTIONS LTD. present

THE JACK ROSE REPERTORY PLAYERS in

"BUT ONCE A YEAR"

By FALKLAND L. CARY

The Cast in order of appearance

Mary Meldon	URSULA CAMM
Ann Meldon (her younger daughter)	PATRICIA WILMOUR
Alice (the Maid)	SHIELA KAY
Topsy Richards (Ann's & Olivia's Aunt)	JOANNA GLASS
Tony Hartley	LEONARD LEWIS
Enid Hartley (his mother)	AGNES POOLEY
Olivia Meldon (Mary's elder daughter)	YOOTHA JOYCE

THE SCENE.—The Lounge in John Meldon's House, "Garlands," in Hartfordshire.

ACT I. The Evening of Xmas Eve.
  10 minutes Interval
ACT II. Xmas Day Afternoon.
  10 minutes Interval
ACT III. Xmas Day Evening.

ACKNOWLEDGMENTS

Treasure Island (THEATRE)
By Robert Louis Stevenson
Role - Unknown

Work & Performance Highlights 1952

The Young In Heart. (THEATRE)
By Derek Benfield
Role – Teenager

ASHTON-UNDER-LYNE

"The Young in Heart" received a warm reception at the Royal recently. Although there is little originality of theme, there is freshness and understanding in the dialogue, and the blend of comedy and sentiment gave full scope to the Jack Rose Repertory Players. Agnes Pooley and Kenneth Keeling played Mr. and Mrs. Purvis with charm and sincerity, and Yootha Joyce, as a lovable teen-ager, and Leonard Lewis, as her Yorkshire suitor, provided most of the laughs. Others in the cast were Joanna Glass, Philip Newman, John Chilvers, Ursula Camm, Patricia Wilmore, and Donald McKillop. The play was produced by Kenneth Keeling.

Heaven And Charing Cross. (THEATRE)
Author Unknown
Role – Unknown

The Happy Marriage. (THEATRE)
By John Clements
Role – Unknown

Work & Performance Highlights 1953

Harry Hanson was known to pressure his actors to always appear glamorous, on and off stage. This filtered through to the other associated Harry Hanson companies. He always insisted his actresses were well turned out, which may explain why Yootha never looked anything but glamorous in public. DEAR YOOTHA… THE LIFE OF YOOTHA JOYCE

Charley's Uncle. (THEATRE)
By Denis Staveley
Role – Sylvia Chisholm

WESTCLIFF

Harry Hanson's Court Players returned fit after some weeks' absence and presented "Accolade" effectively under Jan Fogarty's capable direction on May 11, with Walter Wingham and Edna Hart riveting attention as Trenting and his wife, and Harry Bowers and Dorrie Tomlinson as Harold and Phyllis fully efficient in their parts. In "Night Call" the same artists were prominent. Peter Lee was also consistently good as Steve, and Paula Flack made an instant success as Miriam. Frederick Horrey built up a cool, calculating figure as the detective, and Grimmond Henderson, the stage director, completed the cast. For the final week of the month "Charley's Uncle" brought laughter into the Whitsun holiday and was rattled through by Dorrie Tomlinson, effervescent as Bubbles, Harry Bowers as Cosher Bennett, Walter Wingham as the much-married vicar, Edna Hart as his "bossy" spouse, Peter Lee as Charley, and Yootha Joyce, a newcomer, who made a palpable hit as Sylvia. For Coronation Week "Our Family" will be staged.

Our Family. (THEATRE)
By Kenneth Watson and Ivan Butler
Role – Elinor Winton

WESTCLIFF

At the Palace during June plays staged by Harry Hanson's Court Players have been of unequal merit, as so often happens with repertory companies with long runs. "Our Family" was a farce that depended on familiar situations and too much of the "strip-tease" element, but Walter Wingham, Frederick Horrey, Paula Flack, Yootha Joyce and Harry Bowers lent distinction to their rôles. In "Queen Elizabeth" Edna Hart dealt ably with the amorous, temperamental and ever-jovial aspects of the character. The high-pitched tones she assumed, however, though they may have been traditional, jarred a little on those who prefer her natural, deeper voice. Harry Bowers made a good impression as the gay Jean de Simier, and Walter Wingham was always effective as François de Valois. Lodge Percy came back for the week to give a fine piece of acting as John Stubbs, and Peter Lee played the Earl of Leicester with some spirit. "Widows are Dangerous" was a really funny farce that had originality in situations and dialogue, and gave many chances for diverting bits of business. The cast of six, all scoring hearty laughter, comprised Edna Hart, Dorrie Tomlinson, Walter Wingham, Yootha Joyce, Peter Lee and Harry Bowers. "Autumn Crocus" was revived on June 22 in a scrupulously well staged and acted presentation, with Harry Bowers and Yootha Joyce in tenderly played love scenes.

Widows Are Dangerous. (THEATRE)
By June Garland Thomas
Role – Angela Lawrence

COURT PLAYERS WELL ESTABLISHED AT WESTCLIFF

WITH the 360th performance approaching, Harry Hanson's Cou Players have certainly established themselves at the Palac Westcliff. They went there first in 1944, and, except for breaks durin which amateurs and an annual pantomime have been in possession, hav remained ever since. The producer has always been Jan Fogarty, whos ability to tackle any kind of play has brought happy results. He is no manager of the company as well, and now and again also plays parts.

Naturally the Players have changed with the years. Some have gon to other Hanson companies, some have found opportunities to bette their positions in London or elsewhere. Of those who remain, Walte

Edna Hart, Walter Wingham, Yootha Joyce, Harry Bowers, Peter Lee and Dorrie Tomlinson in Jan Fogarty's production of "Widows Are Dangerous"

Wingham and Minnie Watersford still offer good work. Miss Watersford is not seen so often, but likes to do an occasional week. Mr. Wingham is usually seen week by week playing one of his character old men. He is a conscientious actor for whom every detail must be exact. Edna Hart has been at the Palace some time, too, and can play almost any part, though she prefers one with some humour in it, and is very popular at Westcliff.

Not many plays of a highbrow kind are presented, though attempts have been made to do so. Shaw and Priestley have been found too talkative to attract. Plays with a good plot and plenty of action appeal more, and a piece with laughter as its basis is always attractive. There are people in Southend and Westcliff who clamour for Shakespeare and some of the old comedies, but the cost of staging these is not obvious to those who desire them. The Players get along very well with their one-scene comedies and an occasional mystery play.

Licensee and General Manager
HERBERT J. POINTER, A.I.M.E.M

PALACE THEATRE
Week Commencing Monday, June 15th, 1953

Theatre Manager
WILLIAM T. TATE, A.I.M.E.M

HARRY HANSON presents The Court Players

IN

"WIDOWS ARE DANGEROUS"
by JUNE GARLAND THOMAS

CHARACTERS IN ORDER OF THEIR APPEARANCE

Louise Kingston	Edna Hart
Brian Maitland	Walter Wingham
Dinah Kingston	Dorrie Tomlinson
David Foster	Peter Lee
Angela Lawrence	Yootha Joyce
George Lawrence	Harry Bowers

The Play is Produced by JAN FOGARTY

Stage Settings painted by ROBERT DALTON

Manager		JAN FOGARTY
Stage Director	For	GRIMMOND HENDERSON
Stage Manager	HARRY HANSON	PAULA FLACK
Stage Carpenter		FRANK CAREY

SYNOPSIS OF SCENES

The action takes place in the living room of Louise's cottage in the country.

ACT I
Late afternoon.

ACT II
One hour later.

ACT III
Next morning.

The Court Players would like to express their appreciation and thanks to the following for their kind co-operation

Antique Furniture by Susan L. Lentland, 353 London Road.
Modern Furniture by S. Blackman, 211 London Road.
R. S. Pateman & Son, 697 London Road and A. Goodman, 35 Queens Road, Southend.
Records by Hodges & Johnson, Pianos, Broadway, Leigh. Silverware by R. A. Jones & Sons Ltd.,
Stage Dressings by Margaret Nourse, 363 London Road. High Street, Southend.
Lamps and Furniture by Benns, Electrical Contractors, 280 London Road.
Shades and Electric Fittings by H. A. Lee, 531 London Road, Westcliff.
Hon. Chiropodist B. J. Williams, L.C.H, 275 Cadnor Avenue.
Stage Confectionery by Harris's Bakers, West Road. Furs by Kippens Furs Ltd, 815 London Road.
Ladies Hats by "Dorothy", 105 Hamlet Court Road. Smiles by Gordon-Morton Grayscale Toothpaste.
Nylon Stockings by Kayser-Bondor. Pictures by The Fairing Shop, 1306 London Road, Leigh.
Cigarettes by Abdulla.

Autumn Crocus. (THEATRE)
By Dodie Smith
Role – The Lady in Spectacles

Music For Murder. (THEATRE)
By John French
Role – Priscilla Hunter

Queen Elizabeth. (THEATRE)
By Hugh Ross Williamson
Role – Lettice, Dowager Countess of Essex

WESTCLIFF

The plays presented by Harry Hanson's Court Players in July were mostly revivals of much interest to those who had seen them elsewhere and to others who could enjoy their fresh treatment by Jan Fogarty as producer. "Music for Murder" had its thrills, especially in the last act. Dorrie Tomlinson had a realistic scream earlier which certainly startled everybody, and Edna Hart was a motherly Mary Wimple. Yootha Joyce shone as Priscilla, Frederick Horrey was a convincing detective, and Peter Lee gave effect to his lines as Ronald. "Born Yesterday" brought Walter Wingham to the fore in a fine study of an American racketeer, and Harry Bowers defined neatly the traits of Eddie. Yootha Joyce was again excellent as Billie, and Paula Flack made much of a small part. "The Outsider" afforded many chances to Peter Lee as the unorthodox healer, and he was ably contrasted by the regular medicos, clearly interpreted by Lodge Percy and others. Once again Yootha Joyce was delightfully sincere as the crippled girl. In "Smilin' Through," Dorrie Tomlinson was dainty as Moonyean. Walter Wingham scored as the old doctor, and Harry Bowers was a romantic young lover. Peter Lee was on unfamiliar ground as the old uncle, but was better in the second act, and Paula Flack's pleasant voice was well used as Mary. Doris Lyndon sang the theme song with clarity between the acts. "Worm's Eye View" was the last of the month's presentations and probably the most amusing. In this gay comedy (originally seen here with Ronald Shiner as Porter in 1945) all the company combined to make merry.

2

Born Yesterday. (THEATRE)
By Garson Kanin
Role – Billie Dawn

The Outsider. (THEATRE)
By Dorothy Brandon
Role – [The Crippled Girl] Lalage Sturdee

Smilin' Through. (THEATRE)
By A.L. Martin
Role – Unknown [Yootha is not listed in the programme]

Worm's Eye View. (THEATRE)
By R. F. Delderfield
Role – Bella, Mrs. Bounty's Daughter

Maiden Ladies. (THEATRE)
By Edward V. Hoile & Guy Paxton.
Role – Valerie Ward

WESTCLIFF

"Maiden Ladies" opened the August list of plays presented by Harry Hanson's Court Players at the Palace, and provided much amusement for holiday audiences with its farcical situations. The chief characters were played by Peter Lee, Harry Bowers, Walter Wingham, Edna Hart, Dorrie Tomlinson and Yootha Joyce. "Murder Mistaken" had Peter Lee in the leading part. Quiet at first, he had his chances in the last act and made effective use of them. Elaine Campbell's pleasant acting as Charlotte was notable, and Yootha Joyce was commendable for artistic work. Hazel Peterson made a good impression as Emmie; Edna Hart, as Monica, was more than efficient, and Frederick Horrey made a good deal of the part of Philip. The company reverted to farce in "Wild Horses," with Walter Wingham leading the way delightfully as George, and Peter Lee as his fellow-conspirator. Elaine Campbell was attractive as Cora, and Yootha Joyce scored once more as Iris. Hazel Peterson was cordially welcomed as the eccentric Mrs. Beebee, and Lodge Percy gave an excellent character-study of Judge Reckam. "Relative Values" was produced with a fine sense of its quality by Jan Fogarty, the manager and producer of each play. Outstanding were Edna Hart, Elaine Campbell, Yootha Joyce, Paula Flack, Walter Wingham, Harry Bowers, Frederick Horrey and Peter Lee.

Murder Mistaken. (THEATRE)
By Janet Green
Role – Freda Jefferies

Wild Horses. (THEATRE)
By Ben Travers
Role – Iris Ingle

"I can imagine when she was in rep she probably played every part going." **TONI PALMER**

"Yootha attended my christening. According to family legend she held me, I cried and she quickly gave me back to my mother saying 'Babies don't like me, darling!'" **MANDY CARR**

Licensee and General Manager
HERBERT J. POINTER, A.I.M.E.M

PALACE THEATRE
Week Commencing Monday, Aug. 17th, 1953
HARRY HANSON presents The Court Players

IN

"WILD HORSES"
by BEN TRAVERS

Theatre Manager
WILLIAM T. TATE, A.I.M.E.M.

CHARACTERS IN ORDER OF THEIR APPEARANCE

Kate Slaughter	Edna Hart
Cora Slaughter	Elaine Campbell
George Slaughter	Walter Wingham
David Barnett	Harry Bowers
Iris Ingle	Yootha Joyce
Trumper Norton	Peter Lee
Mrs. Beebee	Hazel Peterson
Kersit	Frank Carey
Louis Beile	Arthur Dallas
Judge Reckam	Lodge Percy
A police sergeant	Frederick Horrey
P.c. Osborne	Grimmond Henderson
P.c. Blood	Jan Fogarty

The Play is Produced by JAN FOGARTY
Stage Settings painted by ROBERT DALTON

Manager .... } .... JAN FOGARTY
Stage Director .... } For { GRIMMOND HENDERSON
Stage Manager .... } HARRY HANSON { PAULA FLACK
Stage Carpenter .... } .... FRANK CAREY

SYNOPSIS OF SCENES

The action of the play takes place in the drawing room of George Slaughter's house, 34 Marquis Street, London, S.W.1.

ACT 1
Early afternoon. A bright summer's day.

ACT II
Scene 1   The same day, 5.30 p.m.
Scene 2   That night.

ACT III
A few minutes later.

The Court Players would like to express their appreciation and thanks to the following for their kind co-operation.

*Antique Furniture by Susan L. Leonard, 333 London Road.
Modern Furniture by S. Blackman, 911 London Road.
R. S. Paternan & Son, 627 London Road and A. Goodman, 84 Queens Road, Southend.
Records by Hodges & Johnson, Pianos, Broadway, Leigh. Silverware by R. A. Jones & Sons Ltd., High Street, Southend.
Stage Dressings by Margaret Broome, 369 London Road.
Lamps and Furniture by "Perrys," Electrical Contractors, 282 London Road.
Shades and Electric Fittings by H. A. Lee, 132 London Road, Westcliff.
Hon. Chiropodist B. I. Williams, L.C.H. 273 Carlton Avenue.
Stage Confectionery by Harris's Bakery, West Road. Furs by Koppens Furs Ltd, 815 London Road.
Ladies Hats by "Dorothy" 105 Hamlet Court Road. Snuffles by Gordon-Moores Cosmetic Toothpaste.
Nylon Stockings by Kayser-Bondor. Pictures by The Framing Shop, 2106 London Road, Leigh
Cigarettes by Abdulla.*

Relative Values. (THEATRE)
By Noel Coward
Role – Mrs. Moxton

Waters Of The Moon. (THEATRE)
By N.C. Hunter
Role – Evelyn Daly

My Wife's Lodger. (THEATRE)
By Dominic Roche
Role – Maggie Ann Higginbotham

WESTCLIFF

September's list of plays presented by the Court Players has covered a wide range. The versatility of the company was evident in "Waters of the Moon," in which Edna Hart and Yootha Joyce gave fine portrayals and Peter Lee played the foreign refugee with understanding. Walter Wingham was happily cast as the retired colonel, and it was good to see Minnie Watersford in one of her rare appearances. Paula Flack, too, did clever work as Mrs. Daly. "My Wife's Lodger" was keenly enjoyed by typical holiday audiences. Walter Wingham, in effective basic set, on which the changes were rung, and the hand of Laurence Payne was obvious in the spectacular sword-fights. In Shirley Cooklin Mr. Winton has discovered a young actress who can encompass passion, tenderness and pathos, and who acts with intelligence. She was an appealing Juliet. The youth of the company generally was appropriate to the play, as Trader Faulkner's Romeo, Geoffrey Taylor's gay and fantastic Mercutio and Robert Crewdson's cold and deadly Tybalt evidenced. The acting honours, however, went to Eileen Beldon, whose Nurse was a rich character study. There was also notably good work by Jack Rodney (Capulet), Judith Gick (Lady Capulet), Michael Hitchman (Friar Laurence) and George Cooper (the Prince).

The Man. (THEATRE)
By Mel Dinelli
Role – Ruth

Licensee and General Manager
HERBERT J. POINTER, A.I.M.E.M

PALACE THEATRE
Week Commencing Monday, Sept. 21st., 1953

Theatre Manager
WILLIAM T. TATE, A.I.M.E.M.

HARRY HANSON presents The Court Players

IN

"RED LETTER DAY"
by ANDREW ROSENTHAL

CHARACTERS IN ORDER OF THEIR APPEARANCE

Toby	Wilfrid Downing
Ned Sutherland	Walter Wingham
Anna	Paula Flack
Alice	Shirley Rogers
Lora Sutherland	Edna Hart
Tim	Harry Bowers
Carol (his wife)	Elisabeth Danby
Jane Cooper	Yootha Joyce
Helen Conrad	Elaine Campbell
Manuel Del Vega	Frederick Horrey

The Play is Produced by JAN FOGARTY

Stage Settings painted by ROBERT DALTON

Manager .... } For { .... JAN FOGARTY
Stage Director .... } HARRY HANSON { GRIMMOND HENDERSON
Stage Manager .... } .... PAULA FLACK
Stage Carpenter .... } .... FRANK CAREY

SYNOPSIS OF SCENES

The action takes place in the upstairs sitting-room in the Sutherlands' house, the East Fifties, New York City.—Early this year.

ACT I
Breakfast.

ACT II
The party.

ACT III
After the party.

Red Letter Day. (THEATRE)
By Andrew Rosenthal
Role – Jane Cooper

I Want to Get Married. (THEATRE)
By Allan Barnes
Role – Annie Worthington

Licensee and General Manager
HERBERT J. POINTER, A.I.M.E.M

PALACE THEATRE
Week Commencing Monday, Sept. 28th., 1953

Theatre Manager
WILLIAM T. TATE, A.I.M.E.M.

HARRY HANSON presents The Court Players

IN

"I WANT TO GET MARRIED"
by ALLAN BARNES

CHARACTERS IN ORDER OF THEIR APPEARANCE

Martha Worthington	Edna Hart
Gibson	Grimmond Henderson
Annie Worthington	Yootha Joyce
Henry Worthington	Walter Wingham
Gladys Worthington	Paula Flack
Bridget O'Sullivan	Elisabeth Danby
Councillor Parkinson	Frederick Horrey
Jacob Ramsbottom	Harry Bowers

The Play is Produced by JAN FOGARTY

Stage Settings painted by ROBERT DALTON

SYNOPSIS OF SCENES

The entire action of the play passes in the lounge of the Mayor of Taunpool's house in the North of England.

ACT I
Scene 1—A Monday morning in September.
Scene 2—Two hours later.
Scene 3—Evening, the same day.

ACT II
Scene 1—The same evening. Two hours later.
Scene 2—Late afternoon. A few hours later.

ACT III
The same evening. Ten minutes later.

The Gift. (THEATRE)
By Mary Lumsden
Role – Lady Elizabeth Crossley

> in a sound presentation of "The Gift," in which Elisabeth Danby showed genuine talent as the blind girl and Walter Wingham was convincing as Sir David Crossley. Minnie Watersford used her long experience to much advantage as the old housekeeper, and Peter Lee, Yootha Joyce and Edna Hart were sincere as the other characters. "The Deep Blue Sea" gripped audiences with some tense acting by Yootha Joyce, Walter Wingham and Peter Lee. In "The Happy Prisoner," Walter Wingham scored as Oliver, Yootha Joyce was properly downright as the farm-girl, and Paula Flack was notably good as Heather.

The Deep Blue Sea. (THEATRE)
By Terence Rattigan.
Role – Hester Collyer

The Happy Prisoner. (THEATRE)
By John McNair
Role – [Farm Girl] Violet North

Daughter of My House. (THEATRE)
By Barry Phelps
Role – Anna

Having A Wonderful Time. (THEATRE)
By Douglas Treverne and Peter Young
Role – Phoebe Tootle (A spinster)

> **WESTCLIFF**
>
> November began at the Palace with Harry Hanson's Court Players in "Having a Wonderful Time." This play has little plot but plenty of slapstick nonsense reminiscent of former times. Still, it gained much laughter. The company seemed to revel in its absurdities and duly fell on the floor (once there were six lying prone) and engaged in other antics. The best of the acting came from Elisabeth Danby, Yootha Joyce, Walter Wingham as a comic parson and Edna Hart as a cheery widow. The following week was devoted to a Delderfield play, "Glad Tidings," a much better piece, in which the humour came naturally from the plot and gave happy opportunities to all concerned. Harry Bowers dealt joyously with his part and Elisabeth Danby was delightful as Jo. Yootha Joyce and Paula Flack played a less youthful couple dexterously, and an older pair were acted with skilled judgment by Edna Hart and Walter Wingham. The officer and corporal from the R.A.F. were merrily delineated by Peter Lee and Grimmond Henderson, and the gardener was effectively treated by Frederick Horrey. The production by Jan Fogarty and the settings by Hubert Forde were both fine achievements. The Players ended their tenth season here on November 14 and opened at the Gaiety, Ayr, on the 16th with "My Wife's Lodger." They will return to Westcliff after the pantomime.

Glad Tidings. (THEATRE)
By R. F. Delderfield
Role – Celia Forester

Wide Boy. (THEATRE)
By Ian Stuart
Role - Clara

"WIDE BOY"

On January 26, at the Regal, was produced a new play by Ian Stuart, "Wide Boy."

Ethel Hawkins	June Bowkley
Bert Hawkins	Ian Stuart
Clara	Yootha Joyce
Gilbert	Angus Neil
Mrs. Maynard	Myra Jacobs
Miss Stratton	Iris Wells
Alfie	Jon Rollason

Produced by the Author.

This is an attempt to show the influence of home-life on teenagers. A typical lower-class London home is shown with Cockney humour and pathos alternating through three well-written acts. Ethel Hawkins has been twice married and has had by her first husband two children who have drifted into wrongdoing. Gilbert, the son, has become a "spiv" and the daughter, Clara, is a sophisticated "good-time girl." Ethel, in her second marriage, has found a strong man who is in the special constabulary and who stands for no nonsense. His own son Alfie, is a young soldier, honest and keen on his duties. When he comes home on leave he does not like the atmosphere and stands by his father. Both Gilbert and Clara speedily find trouble, the former being attacked and robbed of stolen money he is carrying, and the latter finding herself visited twice by a probation officer. The "wide boy" has every prospect of becoming a criminal, but the "old man" (his step-father), after talking sternly to him and finding him still recalcitrant, takes off his belt and is on the point of giving the lad some much-needed corporal punishment as the curtain falls.

This outspoken play is worth studying by everybody, whether interested in juvenile delinquency or not. Ian Stuart, the author, has staged it effectively and also plays the righteous father with fine judgment.

Angus Neil makes a sound impression, too, as the "spiv," and Jon Rollason, as the younger son, acts well. Yootha Joyce, as the sullen yet graceful Clara, is always true to life, and June Bowkley is convincing as the worried mother.

Work & Performance Highlights 1955

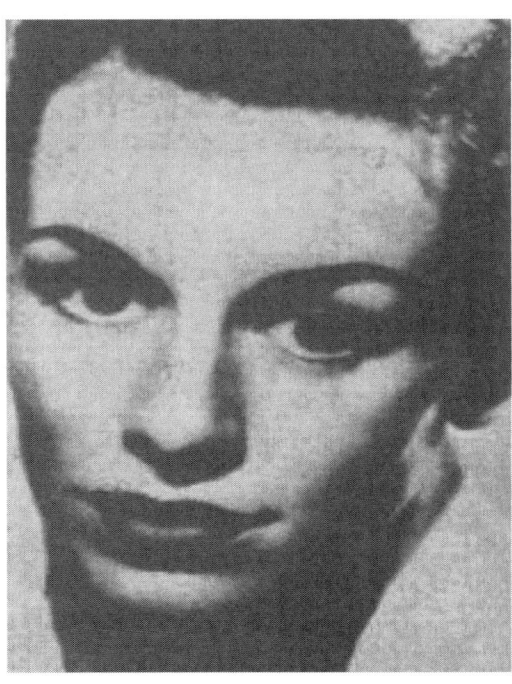

"I fancied myself as Judy Garland, and started singing 'I was born in a trunk' in the empty theatre, on the edge of the stage. - I got so carried away that I fell off the stage into the pit and sprained my ankle." YOOTHA JOYCE

Murder at the Vicarage. (THEATRE)
By Agatha Christie
Role - Anne Protheroe

Call of the Flesh. (THEATRE)
By Rex Howard Arundel
Role - Stella Loman

WOLVERHAMPTON HIPPODROME (re 1).—" Call of the Flesh "—Glyn Edwards, Yootha Joyce, Ivor Salter, etc.

PRESTON HIPPODROME. — " Call of the Flesh "—Glyn Edwards, Yootha Joyce, Ivor Salter, etc.

Sam Linfield, etc.
BOSCOMBE HIPPODROME (re. 1).—" Call of the Flesh "—Glyn Edwards, Yootha Joyce, Ivor Salter, etc.

SWANSEA EMPIRE (re. 12).—" Call of the Flesh "—Glynn Edwards, Yootha Joyce, Ivor Salter, etc.

"Rex Arundel's Vile Inheritance, *later renamed* The Call of the Flesh, *was a terrible show -all about venereal disease. It was popular because at that time the theatre was very puritanical; and of course you had the Lord Chamberlain's rulings, where you were only allowed to say 'bloody' twice, but it was considered by the standards of the time to have been a little bit naughty. We did very well with it, actually, but I had to recast at one point for the part of a hooker from London. Yootha auditioned, and in fact I auditioned two ladies, who both performed very well. Yootha wanted £12 a week as her fee, whereas the other actress said she would do it for £10 a week. So I thought to hell with the expense, and employed Yootha. She was a lovely lady. She read the part very well, and looked very sexy on stage, in everything, and she'd been very successful in the Harry Hanson Players. I took her on, so I must have fancied her. She was quite a girl. We went on tour and we hung out together. There wasn't much to do in the afternoons, so we just sort of slid into bed together."*
GLYNN EDWARDS

CITY VARIETIES LEEDS

Telephone 30808/9 — Manager and Licensee: PIP PAWSON, 25, Moynihan House, The Flats, Leeds 9 — Box Office Open Daily

6.15 | MONDAY, AUGUST 8TH, | 8.15
Matinees Tuesday & Saturday at 2.30

LONDON'S MOST DARING PLAY

GLYN EDWARDS PRODUCTIONS PRESENT
R. HOWARD ARUNDEL'S
SENSATIONAL STORY OF CRIME IN OUR STREETS

CALL OF THE FLESH

NAKED!!! RAW!! GRIPPING! — A MUST —

WITH
REX DEERING
YOOTHA JOYCE
WILLIAM RIDOUT
MARK BRACKENBURY
GLYN EDWARDS
PATRICIA IVEY
DEREK ROYLE
JOAN BERRINGER
AND
IVOR SALTER

UNDER THE PERSONAL DIRECTION OF REX DEERING

ADULTS ONLY!

"The play turned out to be so popular that I took it on tour: it ran until the panto season. After the run, however, I never produced again and went straight into the acting profession, and did that for the rest of my life. After it finished, I joined the renowned Theatre Workshop, with Joan Littlewood. Yootha joined a few months later." GLYNN EDWARDS

"Yootha was very competitive, - She was fussy too. I remember when we were together; she went up for a role in Agatha Christie's *The Mousetrap*, *the famous long-running play. I know she was offered a role in that. We'd only been together for a very short while and we were also pretty poor. She went to see it, read the script and said no. She wouldn't do anything just to be in work." GLYNN EDWARDS

Work & Performance Highlights 1956

Good Soldier Schweik. (THEATRE)
By Jaroslav Hašek.
Role - Unknown (Small part)

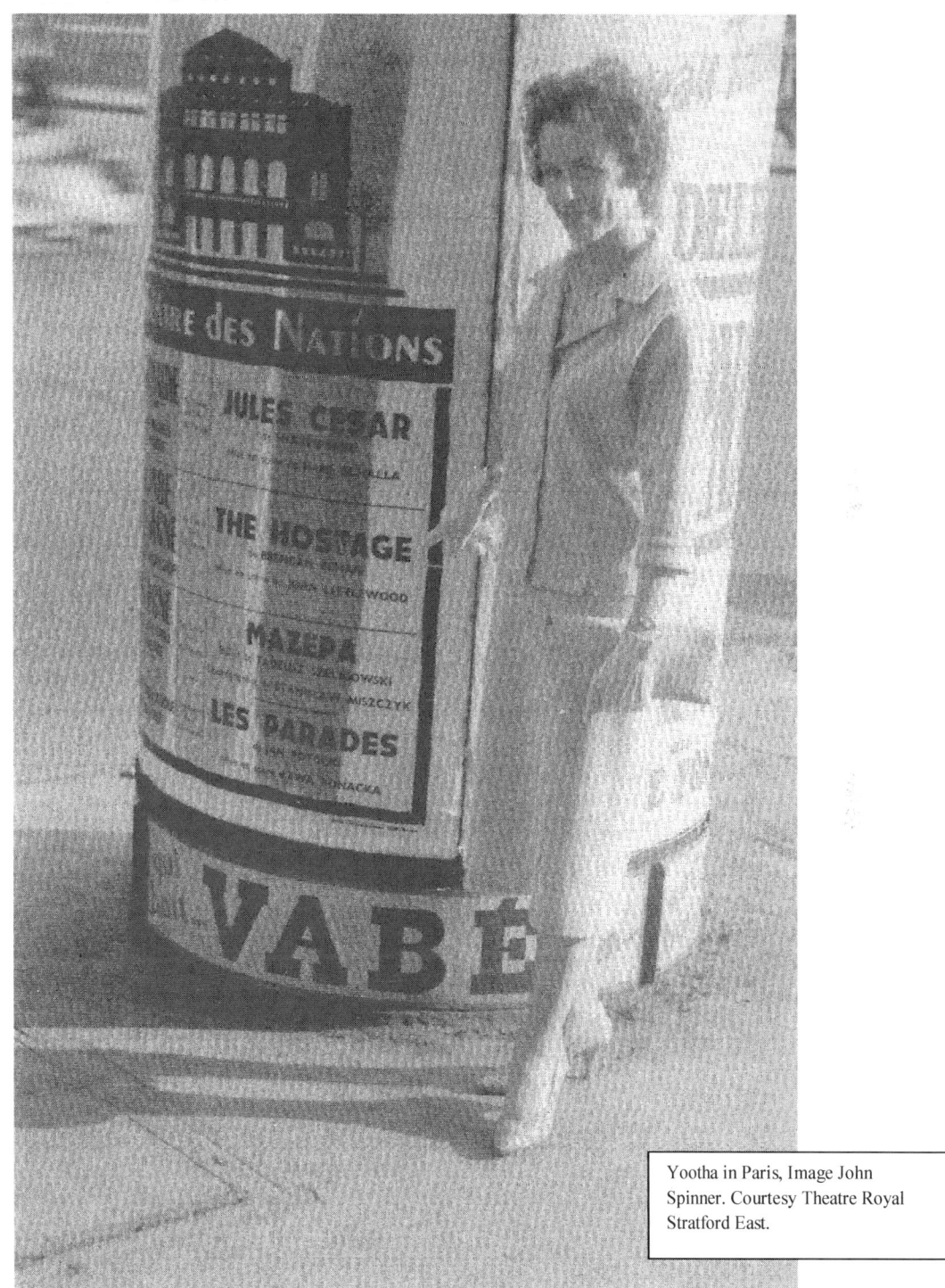

Yootha in Paris, Image John Spinner. Courtesy Theatre Royal Stratford East.

Yootha's handling of her small role - Some said that it made a distinct impression on Joan Littlewood, who believed Yootha was "a great comedienne," With this in mind, she asked Yootha to join the company on its return to Stratford, "the one in the East End darling, not the one on Avon" Yootha once quipped; she thought this request from Joan was "lovely." **DEAR YOOTHA... THE LIFE OF YOOTHA JOYCE**

Yootha (far left) at rehersals
Image John Spinner. Courtesy
Theatre Royal Stratford East.

Captain Brassbound's Conversion (THEATRE)
By George Bernard Shaw
Role - House Manager

Treasure Island. (THEATRE)
By Robert Louis Stevenson
Role - House Manager

Playboy of the Western World (THEATRE)
By John Millington Synge
Role - Susan Brady

Yootha (above) in Playboy of the Western World. Image John Spinner. Courtesy Theatre Royal Stratford East.

"January 1957, Yootha took on the role of Susan Brady in John Millington Synge's Playboy of the Western World, *which played at Stratford for three weeks. It was an ambitious play to attempt, particularly because of the strange, rather artificial Irish English that it's written in. Reviews were not great.* The Daily Telegraph *review was headlined "The Playboy Lacks Poetry" and called it an "uninspired revival."* The Times *was particularly harsh on some cast members, and noted that "Theatre Workshop's approach to Synge is that of a company who modestly doubt their capacity to deal with his speech rhythms. They hope to make up for the deficiency by sheer acting; but it is, of course, a fatal deficiency."*
DEAR YOOTHA… THE LIFE OF YOOTHA JOYCE

The Duchess of Malfi (THEATRE)
By John Webster
Role - Julia

'THE DUCHESS OF MALFY'
Revival of play by John Webster. Presented at the Royal, Stratford, E., on February 21. Costumes by Josephine Wilkinson.
Ferdinand, Duke of Calabria .. Philip Locke
The Cardinal .... Howard Goorney
Antonio Bologna .. Glynn Edwards
Delio. .... Peter Smallwood
Daniel de Bosola .... Dudley Foster
Castruccio .... Barry Clayton
Marquis de Pescara .... David Case
Lord Silvio .... Brian Murphy
Count Malateste .... Barry Clayton
Doctor .... Brian Murphy
Antonio's son .... Jo Benson
The Duchess of Malfy..Avis Bunnage
Cariola .... Eileen Kennally
Julia .... Yootha Joyce
Directed by John Bury.

By Candlelight. (THEATRE)
By Harry Graham
Role - Unknown

"My first meeting with Yootha, - I came here to the Theatre Royal in 1957 and my very first job was painting the foyer. I was up a ladder one cold morning; I was painting the gold on the filigree and suddenly this figure in a two piece sunflower yellow suit with trousers and high heeled shoes, which was new and rare combination in those days, said, 'morning luv, you're the new dogsbody are you?' I said 'yes, I was just painting the foyer.' 'Yes well the whole place needs a coat of paint, and until they can afford it, they'll have to put up with me - make sure they don't grind you into the ground.'-She just glided into rehearsal of Celestina, [the fifteenth-century Spanish play about a madam]. I was very impressed," MURRAY MELVIN

Yootha mentally, not physically, always had an arm round me, and that's why I would always get the lift home in the bubble car. 'How are you getting home?' she would ask, because we'd be around until about 1 o'clock in the morning, 'Glynn', she would shout, 'we're taking him home.'" MURRAY MELVIN

"I'm desperately conscious of my appearance and I'll go to rehearsals in false eyelashes, the lot. I don't care if false eyelashes are out of fashion. I hardly have eyes, let alone lashes." And again: "I like clothes, but I don't work to a style. I'm inclined to be overdressed rather than underdressed." YOOTHA JOYCE

Work & Performance Highlights 1957

Macbeth (THEATRE)
By William Shakespeare
Role - House Manager

Work & Performance Highlights 1958

Celestina. (THEATRE)
By Fernando de Rojas
Role - Lucrezia

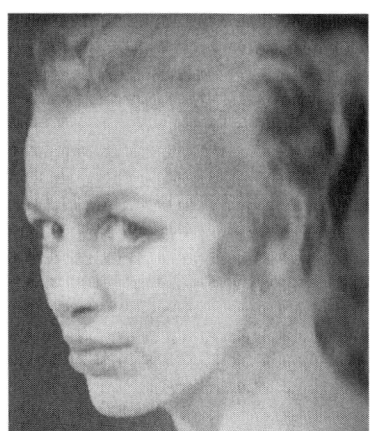

Man, Beast & Virtue (THEATRE)
By Luigi Pirandello
Role - House Manager

THEATRE ROYAL

ANGEL LANE, STRATFORD, E.15

Licensee	JOHN BURY
General Manager	GERALD C. RAFFLES
House Manager	YOOTHA JOYCE

Box Office open from 10.30 a.m.
(Miss Monica Patterson)

(Telephone: MARYLAND 5973/4)

Prices: 7/6, 5/-, 3/6, 2/6, 1/6

Theatre Workshop

presents

man, beast, and virtue

by LUIGI PIRANDELLO

Translated by Edward Eager
Produced by France Jamnik

MONDAY to FRIDAY 8 p.m.   **SATURDAY 5 and 8 p.m.**

The Respectful Prostitute (THEATRE)
By Jean-Paul Sartre
Role - Lizzie

"Joan thought Yootha's best performance, which she directed her in, was as the respectable prostitute in the play by Jean Paul-Sartr,e opposite James Booth." **PETER RANKIN**

Yootha in The Respectful Prostitute. With James Booth. Image John Spinner. Courtesy Theatre Royal Stratford East

"The company did their best with Sartre's play -The prostitute was very justly drawn by Miss Yootha Joyce." THE TIMES

Yootha played Lizzie, a white prostitute who witnesses a crime committed against a black man. As a result, she comes under enormous pressure. It's a real challenge of a part. Glynn Edwards told me "she was good in that, one of her greatest performances. We were both in that show and I was 27 at the time, I'm now 82! So forgive me if I can't remember too much about it. My character was involved in all this awful business with the Klu Klux Klan, and he was about to be lynched! Her customer, I remember, was played by Jimmy Booth. There was a bit of a conflict within a scene as she had me hidden in the room with the customer!" Murray Melvin remembered being really taken aback with her performance, and told me that she became "something else" – "alive sexually," he added. "It was strange to see such a transcendent performance, it was remarkable." He also admitted that "Apart from playing prostitutes, Yootha didn't play many leading parts at Theatre Workshop." DEAR YOOTHA…THE LIFE OF YOOTHA JOYCE

A Christmas Carol. (THEATRE)
By Charles Dickens
Role 1. - Ghost Of Christnas Past
Role 2. - Mrs Trossit

Yootha as Mrs Trossit with Howard Gourney and James Booth. Image Courtesy Theatre Royal Stratford East.

"I'd say Yootha was quite a mover and shaker in those days." **JOY JAMESON**

"I suppose everyone expected us to marry. It was more important twenty years ago. I must have thought I was in love when I married. I remember standing in the registry office and looking at Glynn and thinking, 'What the hell have I done?' Glynn would say exactly the same." **YOOTHA JOYCE**

Yootha and Glynn. Just Married. Image Glynn Edwards.

"We drove to the event in our trusty little bubble car. Yootha couldn't drive herself. We used it as our wedding car and had a few pictures taken getting into it. We would have to be careful if we'd parked it up and not left enough room, because as you know with those cars, the door opened from the front, so sometimes we couldn't get in! So you had to be very careful that people didn't back up to you." **GLYNN EDWARDS**

Work & Performance Highlights 1959

Fings Aint Wot They Used T'be. (THEATRE)
By Frank Norman [Cast recording on CD. Hallmark (2011)]
Role 1. - Murtle
Role 2. - The Brass Upstairs
Role 3. - Policewoman

Yootha (above right) with the rest of the cast of 'Fings' Image Jeff Vickers. Courtesy Theatre Royal Stratford East.

"When Yootha was at Stratford East – unhappily before my time with her, in spite of the fact that I already represented Murray Melvin – it seems to me, discussing those times with Murray, that they had a heck of a good time down there although they'd have been paid tuppence and a toffee apple." JOY JAMESON

"Yootha was 'real', that was the greatest thing about her. I used to love her because she would always slightly take the mickey out of everything. Before we went on to perform once, there was somebody rambling on on stage, and she said 'Oh God, another great speech bites the dust.'" DUDLEY SUTTON

"Yootha was always up for a good time, and would always attract attention. - She would always have plenty of admirers. - She had good sense, you know? Yootha was kind, generous and warm. She knew about life, and would get me out of trouble with girls. She was like a mum in a way, so if I had gotten into trouble with some girlfriend, Yootha would sort it out. She just looked after us. She was like a den mother. Oh! And she loved a good gossip!" DUDLEY SUTTON

"Joanie would stand there in the rehearsal. It would be all theoretically working as a democratically run company… like fuck it was!" TERENCE LEE DICKSON

"I had seen a lot of their productions as a young lad. Miss Joan Littlewood was clearly control-minded. She would sometimes not attend rehearsal; if it was a Tuesday morning, she would simply walk out the room, and according to Yootha, that was the day when she regularly went off to some expensive West End hairdresser and have the full bit done. Then she'd return in the afternoon with a woolly bonnet pulled over her head, and if you ever see photographs of Joanie, you see a woolly bonnet. Next time you look at one just remember how much money went into that haircut. This was at the time when the theatre was making no money. Yootha was in the box office; when she wasn't cast in something she'd be put there, sometimes selling programmes. Everybody had a pop at everything because there was work that needed to be done and they simply couldn't afford people to do it!" TERENCE LEE DICKSON

"I think Yootha fell under the Joan Littlewood spell just like everybody else did. She was very polite about the experience at Theatre Workshop. Yootha told me that there was no money in the box office to pay the wages as it had just been spent on electricity to get the lights on."

" There's something about villainy, professional villainy, that loves being around performers. Gerry Raffles would keep the bar open for these people at Stratford after closing – this was well before the liberalisation of licensing hours. Yootha told me that they hadn't paid the brewery for a while, so there weren't any deliveries from the brewers, and apparently some of the local villains or 'faces' as they were known in those days, got wind of this and said "can't be avin' this, no beer in this bar?" Then suddenly, deliveries were made: nobody knows how this was resolved, but I have a view! But when all's said and done, Stratford was a fantastic place, the shows I saw there were great and many went on, successfully transferring into the West End of London." TERENCE LEE DICKSON

Yootha (Left) as The Policewoman in 'Fings'. Image Jeff Vickers. Courtesy Theatre Royal Stratford East.

"Joan (Littlewood) told me that Yootha was plagued by her mother who would taunt her by saying that she would never make anything of herself as an actress." **PETER RANKIN**

The Hostage. (THEATRE)
By Brendan Behan
Role - Colette

"Brendan Behan was in London with the transfer of The Hostage *to the Wyndham's Theatre. He would have a few beers in the Round Table next door, then he would get into the back of the auditorium and start making fun of people, all because he was pissed. Brilliant authors aren't necessarily nice people to know, and sometimes 'a word' needs to be had. One way Yootha and the company would learn to deal with Behan was to go down to the auditorium and invite him up to sit on stage with them. Whilst there, they'd feed him drink to keep him quiet, of course what a result! I totally approve of this. Speaking as a stage manager, I certainly would have encouraged that. Of course there would be those who would be making a complaint, but I never saw it happen. I can imagine the audience wouldn't have known what was going on, but I'm sure they would have loved it."* TERENCE LEE DICKSON

The Dutch Courtesan. (THEATRE)
By John Marston
Role - Mistress Mulligrub

A PLAY like "The Dutch Courtesan," now at the Royal, Stratford, makes one realise just how far above his contemporaries Shakespeare was. It is also necessary to point out that because a play is seldom performed and is over three hundred years old it is not necessarily good.

The main interest to be derived from "The Dutch Courtesan" is that of a slice of social history. Marston, like most of the old dramatists, was a man of the world presents them to us in a matter-of-fact way which suggests an eager grasping of life, without our modern inhibitions and neuroses. Furthermore, the play employs an earthy language and crude metaphor which is often amusing and, incidentally, shows how much one can get away with under the guise of "culture."

The fact that chiefly distinguishes Marston from his better-known contemporaries is that he was no poet. The serious scenes are regrettably tedious, but these are fortunately few. Nor were Marston's plots brilliant, if this example is anything to go by. "The Dutch Courtesan" is one of those absurd affairs involving young gallants, rapacious merchants and wronged bawds, the whole thing having about as much drama as a Crazy Gang sketch.

'THE DUTCH COURTESAN'

Revival of play by John Marston. Presented by Theatre Workshop at the Royal, Stratford, E.15, on April 24. Setting by John Bury, costumes by Margaret Bury.

Master Mulligrub	Glynn Edwards
Mistress Mulligrub	Yootha Joyce
Cockledemoy	Howard Goorney
Freewill	James Booth
Malheureux	Richard Harris
Caqueteur	Dudley Sutton
Tysefew	Edward Caddick
Mary Faugh	Rachel Roberts
Franceschina	Ann Beach
Beatrice	Carmel Cryan
Crispinella	Stella Riley
Holifernes	Brian Murphy
Nurse Putfer	Leila Greenwood
Master Burnish	Brian Murphy
Constables and Servants	Clive Barker, Dudley Sutton, Roy Barnet, Joe Lloyd
Sir Lionel Freewill	Brian Murphy

Directed by Joan Littlewood

STRENGTH OF COMEDY

A lesser company than Theatre Workshop would, one feels, come hopelessly to grief in this play. In this production Joan Littlewood has slashed her usual ruthless way through the dead wood and has done her best to bring out the strength of the comedy. Under-rehearsal was evident on the opening night, but players with the experience of Rachel Roberts, Yootha Joyce, Howard Goorney, Glynn Edwards and Brian Murphy should have little difficulty in tightening up their scenes. Richard Harris is disappointing as the romantic hero and so is Ann Beach, whose breathlessness in the title-rôle is probably caused by John Bury's setting, the floor of which has a gradient to tax anybody's strength. P.H.

"Yootha's responses in The Dutch Courtesan were incredible. She was playing this rude Elizabethan-type landlady, so her tits were on display. I was playing the gauche young boy, so she was sticking the tits out into me all the time and they just made me cry out whoorrrrr!, which normally I wouldn't have done! I loved that honesty and directness in her performance. Yootha was an inspiration. - She was an absolute joy to be on stage with." DUDLEY SUTTON

In May 1959, the company revived John Marston's **The Dutch Courtesan**, *from 1604. Their first production – according to Murray Melvin, the first for three hundred years – had been put on four years earlier. Joan was the producer, and Glynn and Yootha took leading roles as Master and Mistress Mulligrub. Other members of the cast were Howard Goorney, Richard Harris, Rachel Roberts, Dudley Sutton, Ann Beach, Carmel Cryan and Brian Murphy. The set was designed by John Bury, and fixed on a gradient. It was "exceedingly easy on the eye and remarkably hard on the actors," according to* **Plays and Players**. *According to* **The Times**, *"Mr John Bury's set, with its raked floor of diagonally aligned cheques, encourages a mannered elaboration, which Miss Yootha Joyce avoids by comic acting based on direct attack." According to the critics, the actors couldn't be heard - again according to* **Plays and Players** *"The overwhelming impression was that the speech was that of a 'mumble school.'" Perhaps it was nerves, but* **The Stage Review** *didn't think so: "Under-rehearsal was evident on the opening night, but players with the experience of Rachel Roberts, Yootha Joyce, Howard Goorney, Glynn Edwards and Brian Murphy should have little difficulty in tightening up their scenes." Praise was evident though: "There was an outstanding performance by Howard Goorney as Cockledemoy, a prototype of Til Eulenspiegel, and excellent work from Yootha Joyce, Glynn Edwards and Rachel Roberts as sundry fruity characters of dubious reputations and fortunes. When the cast have looked at the script more carefully, this play richly deserves a transfer." DEAR YOOTHA…THE LIFE OF YOOTHA JOYCE*

Yootha with Murray Melvin. Imaage John Spinner. Courtesy Theatre Royal Stratford East.

Work & Performance Highlights 1960

Fings Aint Wot They Used T'be. (THEATRE)
[West End Transfer]
By Frank Norman
Role 1. - Murtle
Role 2. - The Brass Upstairs
Role 3. - Policewoman

TOSHER COMES TO TOWN

James Booth as Tosher, with Barbara Windsor, Yootha Joyce and Toni Palmer, in a scene from Joan Littlewood's production of "Fings Ain't Wot They Used T'Be", the new musical which is at the Garrick following a season at the Royal, Stratford, E.15. See notice on page 17.

Yootha (left) as Murtle. Image Courtesy Theatre Royal Stratford East.

"Joan admired Yootha for one of her performances in Fings Ain't Wot They Used T'Be. *She played a "Mystery" who didn't speak but just arrived with a client and led him upstairs, her black tasselled dress swishing to and fro, while every one else looked on."* **MURRAY MELVIN**

"Yootha was very funny, she never seemed to realise how good she was. She said to me once, 'I always think the current job will be my last, and I'll never get another' **TONI PALMER**

FINGS IS BUZZIN' AT THE GARRICK IN SOHO SAGA
Street-walkers

Originally seen at the Royal, Stratford, E.15 on February 17, 1959, revived and there is a revised form on January 15, 1960.

Frederick Cochran	Glynn Edwards
Lily Smith	Miriam Karlin
Paddy	Paddy Joice
Sergeant Collins	Tom Chatto
Policewoman	Yootha Joyce
Police Constable	George Sewell
Betty	Toni Palmer
Rosie	Barbara Windsor
Tosher	James Booth
Redhot	Edward Caddick
The Brass Upstairs	Yootha Joyce
Horace Seaton	Wallas Eaton
Gamblers and Builders	Michael O'Brien, Rick Morgan, Louis Adams, Neville Munroe, George Sewell
Percy Fortesque	Wallas Eaton
Myrtle	Yootha Joyce
Busker	George Sewell
Teddygirls and Boys	Margaret Russell, Mary Sheen, Caryll Zeigler, Norman Gunn, James Dark, Tamba Allen
A "Mystery"	Mary Sheen
A Priest	Wallas Eaton

Directed by Joan Littlewood.

Toni Palmer and Barbara Windsor, as the street-walkers, give some indication of what would happen if Ethel Merman and Diana Dors decided to team-up as a sister act. Yootha Joyce, known as "the Brass Upstairs", swings her black fringe with real professional showmanship. Wallas Eaton makes three appearances, his precious interior decorator being the most successful; Glynn Edwards as the ex-razor king, James Booth as the Student Ponce, Edward Caddick as the kleptomaniac with an overcoat that covers a multitude of sins, must be singled out for their penetrating characterisations of Soho types that have to be seen to be believed.

Miss Littlewood has drawn a genuine performance from every member of her cast, even from the less conspicuous teddyboys and girls who slink against the peeling walls of this corner of Soho. Here is a British musical which is first-rate entertainment and one of which we should be duly proud, in that it owes nothing to New York or Vienna. It has been born and bred in London, where it is likely to live for a long time to come.

ERIC JOHNS.

TAILORED MUSIC

Notice should also be taken of Toni Palmer and Barbara Windsor, as Tosher's girls. Tom Chatto, as the police sergeant to whom "dropsy" is an integral part of his income, Edward Caddick, in a wonderful study of a nervous thief, and Yootha Joyce, in three well-contrasted studies. The composer, whose music and lyrics are magnificently tailored for the job, makes a fleeting but hilarious appearance as a busker.

P.H.

Between 17th February and 2nd April, and Yootha took two roles, "a tough policewoman" and "Murtle", playing it up as posh. It was the beginning of fame for Theatre Workshop. The reviews describe Littlewood as "one of the truly heroic spirits in the London theatre;" "she knows how to get the best out of actors and plays alike." Yootha was singled out for praise: she "holds the eye whenever she appears" noted The Observer.

Yootha played her three parts, a brass, Murtle, and a policewoman. A review in The Stage *noted they were "three well constructed studies."* DEAR YOOTHA...THE LIFE OF YOOTHA JOYCE

Yootha (centre) and the cast of 'Fings' Image Courtesy Theatre Royal Stratford East

"Yootha was brilliant as the tough policewoman in Fings: *that performance even scared me. I respected her abilities and strengths as a professional actress. You know, she would drive us mad at times. I remember us all working hard, slogging our guts out, and trying to make something funny. Then she would appear; come down the stairs, say her line, and wallop! Job done. Everything about her seemed so effortless; this lady knew what she was doing. She could play anything, any role, housewife or prostitute. She could be so sexy."* **BARBARA WINDSOR**

The Hostage. (THEATRE)
By Brendan Behan [West End Transfer]
Role - Colette

Work & Performance Highlights 1961

Fings Aint Wot They Used T'be. (THEATRE)
[West End Transfer]
Role 1. - Murtle
Role 2. - The Brass Upstairs
Role 3. – Policewoman

"I tell you this, everybody that worked at Stratford, all came out with a wonderful level of self-confidence, and was that because the old boot that ran the place was a pain in the arse? Probably." **TERENCE LEE DICKSON**

Work & Performance Highlights 1962

Brothers in Law (TV)
- Separation Order
Role - Mrs. Trench
29/05/62

"It was her performance in Fings which so impressed me. It was an amazingly entertaining show with, I think, a first rate cast, from which Yootha Joyce absolutely shone." DENIS NORDEN

"When Frank Muir and Denis Norden saw the show, I got my first television work, in Brothers in Law [a sitcom starring Richard Briers]. - From then on, people just phoned up" YOOTHA JOYCE

Benny Hill (TV)
By Dave Freeman
Episode 2 - Cry of Innocence
Role – Bella
07/12/62

(NB: Not Featuring Yootha Joyce)
Living Today (TV) Features **Yootha Rose** (the woman Yootha was named after)
Around and About the Home *with Richard Waring, including Conrad Phillips ' Hobby Home-made wine, The World of Toys"* *
27/11/62

Crime Lawyer (RADIO)
By Ernest Dudley
14/09/62

Armchair Theatre (TV)
- The Fishing Match (1962)
Role – Cissy

☆ "The Fishing Match" on Sunday August 5th is the second story in playwright Norman King's trilogy of North-Midland life, featuring the same riverside public house as his recent "Night Stop". Starring Kenneth Griffith and Peter Butterworth, and introducing redheads Yootha Joyce and Jo Robottom. Directed by Alan Cooke.

"THE FISHING MATCH" is the title of ABC's Armchair Theatre comedy for Sunday, 19th August. This is the second story in Norman King's Midlands trilogy of which the first play "Night Stop" was screened earlier this summer.
Jo Rowbottom, Colin Campbell and Yootha Joyce play three people stranded in a riverside pub during a summer storm.

was sensitive, and the characterisations were all excellent, and worthy of special mention —a Katherine Hepburn-type Kath (Jo Rowbottom), Cissy (Yootha Joyce) and Reuben (Kenneth Griffith).

Z Cars (TV)
- Full Remission (1962)
Role - Clara Smales

Fings Aint Wot They Used T'be. (THEATRE)
Role - Assistant Director – Manchester

Sparrers Can't Sing (FILM)
Role - Barmaid

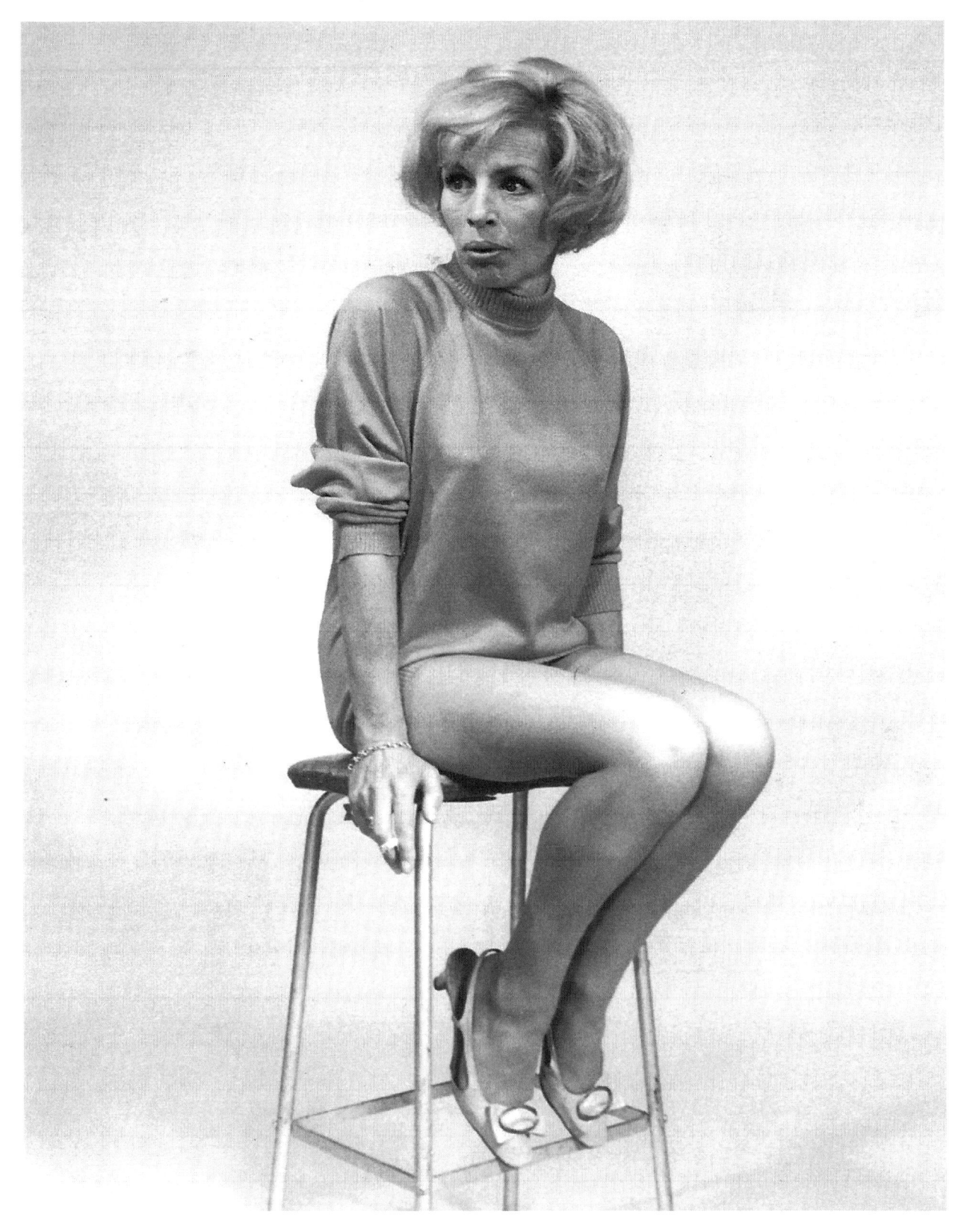

"I remember Yootha mentioned her famous sweater girl picture, where they spent time dressing her up. She pulled that picture out for me one time, I remember, and said "look what they tried to do to me when I was a kid; they tried to make me into a sexy version of Barbara Windsor."" **TERENCE LEE DICKSON**

Work & Performance Highlights 1963

Benny Hill (TV)
Episode Mr. Apollo
By Dave Freeman
Role - Elvira Crudd
03/09/63

> BENNY HILL returns to BBC tv this Tuesday with the first episode in his new series. The six programmes will be situation comedies with Benny Hill assuming a different character for each.
>
> Appearing with Benny in the first episode, "Mr. Apollo", are Yootha Joyce, Graham Stark, Anthea Wyndham and Anna Gilchrist. In following editions Benny will play an electrician's mate, a theatrical dresser, and a farm labourer.
>
> The series has been written by Dave Freeman and is produced by John Street who has been working on "It's A Square World" with Michael Bentine.

"Yootha really wanted to do 'legit' theatre and I wouldn't say Benny Hill's show quite fell into that category. So I don't think she enjoyed it that much. And Benny could be difficult to work with at times." CHRISTINE PILGRIM

Star Parade (TV)
By Benny Hill
30/05/63

Steptoe & Son (TV)
The Bath
By Alan Simpson & Ray Galton
Role - Delia
10/01/63

Comedy Playhouse (TV)
Impasse
By Alan Simpson & Ray Galton
Role - Mrs. Spooner
13/08/63

Comedy Playhouse
Impasse
Bernard Cribbins
and
Yootha Joyce
in tonight's motoring morality
AT 8.20

Comedy Playhouse (TV)
A Clerical Error
By Alan Simpson & Ray Galton
Role – Rita
02/04/63

Inspector Scott Investigates (TV)
By John P. Wynn
(*"A series of crime stories in which listeners can also play the sleuth"*)
07/01/63

A Place to Go (FILM)
Role - Bit Role (uncredited)

Corrigan Blake (TV)
The Removal Men
Role – Abigail

Z Cars (TV)
The Main Chance
Role - Mrs. Gilroy

Yootha's Basement flat as it is today.

Work & Performance Highlights 1964

Story Parade (TV)
 - A Travelling Woman
By John Wain
Role - Ruth Cowley
03/07/64

BBC-2, July 3

THE article about this play in the *Radio Times* described George Links as a man with a psychological urge to grumble. Any man could have told him what was up and the cure for this ailment.

This was a comedy with a bitter core—a bedroom farce with a sour taste.

There were three married couples in the mix-up, its main theme being that if a husband cannot play the man, then the wife is free to find a man who can. And if the wife cannot play the woman, ditto. And so George has an affair with Ruth, George's wife has an affair with Fredric and of the third married couple, Barbara's naughty roving eye is fixed on George. Barbara's husband Evan and Ruth's husband Edward were left just watching this orgy of adultery and had no fun at all.

This was in many ways a difficult play for the actors, because none of the characters were real. They were slightly distorted. It was like looking through a cracked looking glass.

The ones who came off best were **John Saunders** as the gay loud-mouthed bachelor friend; **Bernard Brown**, the erring husband for maintaining his air of intense seriousness; and **Carmel McSharry** and the mute **Fred Hugh** who didn't approve of such goings-on.

BILL EDMUND

CAST

Janet Links .... Jane Downs
George Links .... Bernard Brown
Fredric Captax .... John Saunders
Landlady .... Jean Gregory
Landlord .... Michael Anthony
Barbara Bone .... Pauline Stroud
Evan Bone .... Roy Hanlon
Mrs. Edwards .... Carmel McSharry
Mr. Edwards .... Fred Hugh
Edward Cowley .... Michael Robbins
Ruth Cowley .... Yootha Joyce
Teddy Cowley .... Paul Waller

Written by John Wain and dramatised by Jeremy Paul. Produced by Eric Tayler and directed by David Bellamy.

Dixon of Dock Green (TV)
Child Hunt
By Eric Paice
Role - Mrs. Gates
29/02/64

Dixon of Dock Green (TV)
The Night Man
By David Ellis
Role - Mabel Davies
26/09/64

Z Cars (TV)
First Foot
Role – Grace

Redcap (TV)
A Town Called Love
Role – Magda

Encore (TV)
Diary of a Young Man /Money
By Troy Kennedy Martin & John McGrath
Role - Mrs. Baggerdagger
15/08/64

ITV Play of the Week (TV)
Gina
Role - Vera Maine

Rediffusion, July 27

UP to the first break this was just another play about homely folk visited by a pools fortune and what the neighbours said to her and what the blokes at the factory said to him.

But from the moment Harry was seriously injured the situation suddenly became fascinating. For it's Gina who's won the money and she's Italian and a devout Roman Catholic. When Harry's life is balanced on the surgeon's knife, her prayers include the pledge that if he is spared all £98,000 will go to charity.

He is and it does. But not before Harry has directed the efforts of various people towards trying to persuade Gina to go back on her holy promise. Harry and Gina, once devoted, are now estranged. Ultimately she offers him herself or the money. It's then he realises you can't buy happiness.

The play's success depends tremendously on the actress playing Gina. She has to: react to the news that she has won £98,000; react to the news that her husband has been seriously injured; suffer anguish in the hospital and all the way through to the end. **Maureen Pryor** was superb.

The supporting cast, whether playing flesh and blood or caricature, were also admirable and Miss Pryor had the advantage of having **Richard Pearson** as her co-star. **Toby Robertson's** direction was crisp and relevant. I liked touches like the use of bigger face close-ups for the unpleasant Kerry Duke.

The climax of the play came with a great burst of romantic music as Gina rushes into Harry's arms. I confess I was moved, and I should like to think this is a tribute to the way Mr. Richardson and his stars played it.

BRIAN DE SALVO

CAST

Gina Spencer .... Maureen Pryor
Harry Spencer .... Richard Pearson
Arthur Lowe .... Freddie Jones
Mr. Utteridge .... Frank Williams
Mr. Divott .... John Barrett
Mrs. Wicker .... Susan Richards
Vera Maine .... Yootha Joyce
Yvonne Carter .... June Brown
Foreman Endor .... John Nettleton
Mike .... Michael Faulkes
Charlie Dype .... Henry Soskin
Victor Blane .... Nicholas Pennell
Nurse .... Sandra Payne
John Dussett .... John Bailey
Kerry Duke .... Gerald Harper
Father O'Neill .... Tony Quinn
Mother Superior .... Athene Seyler
Sister Therese .... Jane McCulloch

Written by Michael Ashe and directed by Toby Robertson.

ITV Play of the Week (TV)
I Can Walk Where I Like Can't I?
Role - The Woman

ITV Play of the Week (TV)
A Tricycle Made For Two
Role 1. - Marilyn
Role 2. - Cecily Tarrant
Role 3. - Jane Willows

The Pumpkin Eater (FILM)
Role – Woman at the Hairdressers

FARNHAM

ALFRED LYNCH, stage, film and radio actor and "pop" singer, is showing another aspect of his versatility now — as producer.

His direction of Monte Douglas' "Signpost To Murder," at the Castle Theatre, Farnham, reveals both imagination and a fresh outlook. He is well served by his cast, which includes Yootha Joyce as the neurotic Sally Thomas, and David Burke as Roy. Excellent sets by Suzanne Billings heighten the dramatic effect, and there has been an enthusiastic reception for this lively and colourful production.

Mr. Lynch is acting as guest-producer while Joan Knight is away on a short holiday in the north of England.

"The part Yootha played, a woman in a hairdresser's, had to be specially written, she said, because in the novel the woman was only mentioned in a letter. As we know, she said she never had to audition; but for this project, it seems she did: "I did do a reading and a screen test for that tiny bit, which people still talk about." DEAR YOOTHA… THE LIFE OF YOOTHA JOYCE

"A performance that got Yootha rave reviews was the hairdresser's scene in The Pumpkin Eater *with Anne Bancroft. She was courageously horrid in it."* PETER RANKIN

Signpost To Murder. (THEATRE)
By Monte Douglas
Role - Sally Thomas

Work & Performance Highlights 1965

Six of the Best (TV)
Charlie's Place
Role – Doris

YOOTHA JOYCE will be in the first of a new ATV comedy series called *Charlie's Place* which stars **Ray Brooks** and is directed by **Shaun O'Riordan**.

Cluff (TV)
The Convict
By Gil North
Role - Flo Darby

The Wednesday Thriller (TV)
The Babysitter
By William Trevor
Role - Mrs. Seam
"Not for the Nervous"
18//08/65

> YOOTHA JOYCE having recorded her episode of *Cluff* for BBC-1, directed by **Philip Dudley**, starts rehearsing a play *The Babysitter* for BBC which is to be directed by **Silvio Narizzano**. Yootha will co-star with **Kenneth Griffith** and the play will be recorded on July 21.

Fanatic/Die Die My Darling (FILM)
Role – Anna

> YOOTHA JOYCE, who recently completed a leading role with Tallulah Bankhead in a film entitled *Fanatic* is currently rehearsing an episode of BBC-1's *Z Cars* which is transmitted on December 30.

Catch Us If You Can (FILM)
Role – Nan

Frankie Howerd (TV)
Episode 6
Role - Drunk Woman
"Stars in a series of unlikely situations"
15/08/65

Theatre 625 (TV)
Portraits from the North: The Nutter
By Alan Plater
Role - Miss Binnington
"First of three plays set in the North"
05/12/65

YOOTHA JOYCE is to play Miss Binnington in **Alan Plater's** play *The Nutter*. Rehearsals start today.

Brilliantly funny Plater
by Marjorie Norris

THE NUTTER, BBC-2, Sunday, December 5

HERE was a feast of enjoyment which, like all well-planned feasts, contained the sweet and the sour, the nourishing protein as well as the frothy dessert. Its beginning and its end held their own special piquancy for everyone who works in television, with **Tristram Jellinek** giving a wickedly accurate performance as a smooth presenter of a documentary about the north—switching on the Sincerity bit with an artfully artless removal of those big spectacles—and finally chairing a "discussion" between **Leader Hawkins**, **Anne Jameson**, and **Richard Mathews** which was a masterpiece of observation from performers and writer **Alan Plater** alike.

and the art and culture that make London a magnet are there as a result of a plundering of the north of its material wealth, its ideas and its men and women of talent, must have hit home to many guilty northerners as well as to complacent southerners like myself.

The cast rose to the challenge. **Milo O'Shea**, in the title role, gave a powerful performance of a visionary who saw a way of making the town enviably different. **Ronald Lacey** played one of those puzzling unnerving characters that seem to have been born in a hidden recess of the author's imagination and to have emerged despite rather than because of his cerebral processes. On the surface uncouth and stupid, Jubb was as frightening as an Elemental.

All the other people in the town were recognisable well-drawn types exaggerated to just the right size. No doubt under the guidance of director **Alan Gibson**, the actors wisely left the exaggerations of dialogue and action to look after themselves and concentrated on playing perfectly straight. The operative word is "perfectly". **Ken Parry, Jeremy Longhurst, Helen Fraser, Mike Pratt, Yootha Joyce**, and **John Cater** gave performances which were all the funnier for the way they steadfastly ignored the absurdity of their own and everyone else's behaviour.

Alan Plater has written a play which is brilliantly funny and peopled with characters that on first acquaintance seem no more than caricatures drawn by a master artist. But it is also a play with a strong allegorical quality which by-passes the ordinary senses of sight and hearing and reaches the subconscious by absorption through the pores. Full understanding is not immediate—but neither is it likely to be immediately forgotten. The reminder that the fine buildings

---

Theatre 625 (TV)
"Try for White"
By Basil Warner
Role - Jane Matthews.
18/04/65

Play sprang to life after a slow and noisy beginning

TRY FOR WHITE   BBC-2, Sunday, April 18

A WIDOWED dressmaker in Cape Town is expecting her 19-year-old son home for a holiday. Her only worry seems to be whether he will accept the vulgar but good-hearted bus conductor with whom she has been carrying on a liaison for the last ten years and whom she hopes to marry soon. She appears as bigoted and heartless towards the coloured population as any woman of her type might be expected to be.

In one dramatically effective moment we discover that her coloured servant is actually her mother, grandmother of the young man they both love and of whom they are so proud. Now we understand and can forgive her apparent hatred of the Cape Coloureds. They represent a life as a second-class citizen that she has escaped from through being able to pass as white. Her house of cards collapses when a jealous woman friend betrays her secret to her lover, who turns from her in loathing.

Try for White by **Basil Warner** is not a very well constructed play. Two important supporting characters appeared and disappeared at the wrong times. The plot hung on the hard-to-swallow premise that Jane could have kept her secret in a neighbourhood where it must have been known to many other Coloureds as well as to her girlhood friend. The beginning was too slow to sustain interest, and director **Alan Gibson** made it seem longer by including a long sequence of a band which belonged more in a travel documentary. He also allowed the need to establish the noisiness of the district to override our need to know what was being said.

Then the play sprang to life when Jane's secret was out. We were confronted with the agonies of mind that must come when the question of colour is a legal issue as well as a social one. All the characters were well drawn and seemed taken from life. No one stood out as a star because, although some had longer parts, all seemed too real to be regarded as leads and supports. **Joss Ackland's** uncouth lout, so demonstrably u n w o r t h y of **Yootha Joyce's** intelligent and desperate Jane, had perhaps the most difficult rôle, calling as it did for enough good nature to make her fond of him yet enough underlying viciousness to make his cruel spurning of her part of a believable whole. **Marda Vanne** as Jane's coloured mother also successfully wedded the subservience of the servant to her contrasting moments of dignity and strength. But **Yootha Joyce**, **Gary Bond**, **Zoë Randall**, **Nan Munro** and **Maxine Holden** all gave striking and moving performances.

Natasha Kroll's setting of decayed splendour in the street contributed greatly to the atmosphere, and Alan Gibson made full use of it in the opening sequence.

The casting of this play was so good as to call for comment. There were just enough facial similarities between those who were related and between those who were supposed to have Malaysian blood to give that extra touch of authenticity.

MARJORIE NORRIS

The Wednesday Play (TV)
"The Confidence Course"
By Dennis Potter
Role - Rosalind Arnold
"Starring Dennis Price and Stanley Baxter"
24/02/65

Steptoe & Son (TV)
"A Box in Town"
01/11/65

STEPTOE AND SON
BBC-1,
Monday, November 15

SO it's goodbye to Albert Steptoe and his son Harold and that room full of junk. Strange it will seem not to see **Wilfrid Brambell** and **Harry H. Corbett** in these familiar roles. This last one was very funny indeed and was helped very considerably by the appearance of **Frank Thornton** as the Frenchman and **Allan Gifford** as the American.

Looking back over all the other good Monday night showings of this latest series, I think that **Yootha Joyce** was one of the funniest girl friends Harry H. Corbett ever had. I wish we could have seen more of this 'romance' and also seen more of **Dudley Foster** who gave such good support when he appeared in one as a political agent. A great pity *Steptoe's* finished. Let us hope they'll be back despite the fact that **Ray Galton** and **Alan Simpson** are still saying no.

YOOTHA JOYCE will be appearing in an episode of BBC-1's *Steptoe and Son*, to be recorded on October 10.

Dixon of Dock Green (TV)
"Forsaking All Others"
By N.J.Crisp
Role – Landlady
19/09/65

Unknown project.

Work & Performance Highlights 1966

George And The Dragon (TV)
"Merry Christmas"
Role – Irma

A Man for All Seasons (FILM)
Role - Averil Machin

The Saint (TV)
"The Russian Prisoner"
Role – Jovanka Milanova

YOOTHA JOYCE is now filming her part of Jovanka Furtseva in an episode called *The Russian Prisoner* in the new series of *The Saint* which is being made by ATV in colour. The director is John Moxey.

*Note incorrect character name!

Love Story (TV)
"The Public Duck"
Role - Mrs. Barker

No Hiding Place (TV)
"Ask Me If I Killed Her"
Role - Hilda Myers

Steptoe & Son (TV)
"The Bonds That Bind Us"
Role – The Girlfriend.
25/09/66

Dixon of Dock Green (TV)
"You Can't Buy a Miracle"
By David Ellis
Role - Joyce Watson
12/03/66
"Police hunt an Army deserter as a man is tried for maiming a child."

The Wednesday Play (TV)
"Little Master Mind"
Role - Miriam Green

One of the best Wednesday plays from BBC-1
BY N. ALICE FRICK

WHO better than a practising barrister to write a play about the law, lawyers and the people they defend or prosecute? If the barrister also possesses humour and wit, as **Nemone Lethbridge** demonstrated she does in *Little Master Mind*, the result is great. Her *Wednesday Play* on BBC-1 on December 14 was a high spot in the series.

The ingredients of her fable would ordinarily be stirred into a serious drama. Take four reprehensible confidence men who extort money from Cypriot shopkeepers. Bring them to justice to see them acquitted by a jury one of whose members has been bribed. See the Cypriot, who was the only one of the victims of extortion with enough courage and faith in British justice to give evidence against the accused, forced out of his shop and out of Britain by terrorist bomb attacks. It isn't funny. But Miss Lethbridge is tough-minded, and can turn such a tale into high comedy without reducing the serious undertones. Also, she shrewdly avoided sentimentality in the love affair between Det-Insp. Latcham (**Jerome Willis**) and pretty novice barrister Polly Gordano (**Diana Hoddinott**).

The tone was comic throughout, but the broadest near-farce was generated through secondary characters: Plantagenet King (**Tommy Godfrey** looking like Edward G. Robinson) and his girl Miriam (**Yootha Joyce**), Albert Stump (**John Woodnutt**), the Judge (**Anthony Newlands** making the most of pompous Bench wit), and Trumper (a star turn for **Bryan Pringle**, surely one of the funniest men around). To name only a few in a rich cross-section from around the Temple, the Old Bailey and the City; every character had his own sharply defined personality and his moment of limelight.

The brothers Barking: **George Sewell, John Porter Davison, Michael Robbins** and **Robert Russell**, were engaging crooks who recalled some of the felicities of the Ealing comedies. **Makki Marseilles** and **Poppy Petrohilos**, who played Costas and his wife Katina, made fine honest Cypriots.

Romantic, persistent, businesslike **Jerome Willis** was an upstanding police detective, and he had his triumph at the end when he once again rounded up the brothers who had slipped through his fingers, for bribing a juror. Diana Hoddinott looked most fetching in her wig; and her self-assurance deserved the comeuppance the Inspector administered.

The music, played by **Mimis Margaritis**, was enhancing, something that can't often be said for background music. **Susan Spence's** designs were fine.

The Wednesday Play (TV)
"The Portsmouth Defence"
By Nemone Lethbridge
Role - Miriam Green
30/03/66

JOHN WOODNUTT and Yootha Joyce are both appearing in *The Portsmouth Defence*, which James MacTaggart is directing for BBC-1 for transmission in the Wednesday Play series. The recording date is March 2.

And Some Shall Have (TV)
Unknown

Stranger in the House (FILM)
Role – Woman at the Shooting Range

"James Mason? I don't think he could have been remotely close to Yootha or she would have told me - she knew I fancied him! But she never mentioned him." JOY JAMESON

"I look like Dracula's daughter, - My face was made by somebody who just didn't care that much - it was thrown together." YOOTHA JOYCE

"Yootha had what I could only respectfully describe as an ugly beauty." BARBARA WINDSOR

Work & Performance Highlights 1967

Ways With Words (TV)
Role - Poor woman
"TV for schools and education, for learning English grammar"
02/67

Harry Worth (TV)
"Four's a Crush"
By Ronnie Taylor
Role - Ingrid
31/10/67

Market In Honey Lane (TV)
"The Birds And The Business"
Role - Unknown

Thirty Minute Theatre (TV)
"Teeth"
By Tom Stoppard
Role – Agnes
"An ingenious little piece. It reminded one of Maupassant".
28/08/67

Charlie Bubbles (FILM)
Role - Woman in Café

"Yootha was typecast in comedy, which was a tragedy, because in a film like Charlie Bubbles *she was cast so 'out of the box' as they'd say today."* JOY JAMESON

Our Mothers House (FILM)
Role - Mrs. Quayle

"Yootha in Our Mother's House *was pretty good; her black gloved hand reaching for the door-chain is pretty scary!"*
NEIL SINYARD

"Yootha Joyce is amusing as a floozy," THE MOTION PICTURE HERALD

Kaliedoscope (FILM)
Role - Museum Receptionist

"Warren Beatty was a great fan of Oh! What A Lovely War *and used to watch the show from the wings at the Broadhurst Theatre on Broadway. He told the actress, Fanny Carby, who was in it, that he was shortly coming to England to make a film and they would all be in it. Fanny said to herself something like: "I've heard that one before." but he was as near as dammit as good as his word. Kaleidoscope, a thriller, had not only Fanny in it, but also Yootha, Stephen Lewis, George Sewell, Murray Melvin, John Junkin and Sean Lynch, all Theatre Workshop actors."* PETER RANKIN

The Avengers (TV)
"Something Nasty in the Nursery"
Role - Miss Lister

Turn Out The Lights (TV)
"A Big Hand for a Little Lady"
Role - Monica Nolan

The Wednesday Play (TV)
"An Officer of the Court"
Role - Miriam Green (a "bird")
20/12/67

Which night club owner will shortly be seen in an acting role in BBC-TV's "Officer of the Court" with Tommy Godfrey, Bryan Pringle and Yootha Joyce?

Yes—it's Jimmy Jacobs again, typecast, he points out, "as a swarthy Jewish night club owner".

And which night club owner still presents no less than six acts nightly in two separate shows?

You're right again. Jimmy has the Darling Sisters, London's busiest act, in his midnight show, with two strippers from his Nell Gwynne Theatre, and an hour later he presents the delectable singing Pat Ferris, the desirable dancing and singing Ingrid Anthofer and the debonair Charlie Davis, most vibrant of vocalists.

And there's good news too from the delicious Janet Montana, who tells me that the gorgeous leg she injured early last summer is on the mend and that she hopes to be dancing—at the Gargoyle of course —in the New Year.

★ ★ ★

SUDDENLY, within the last few months, the east side of Leicesbooks, raked in more cash and took himself and bird (**Yootha Joyce**) down to a mansion on the south coast, which he had bought not knowing it was next to a projected open air prison, the very prison Plantagenet himself was destined to end up in.

Tommy Godfrey played Plantagenet and dominated the whole play. His bland face, bouncy self-confident strut and sharp East London twang made for a likeable rogue who carried the play along with great verve.

Comedy blended into tragedy —although this was not too heavily stressed — in the character of Trumper, Plantagenet's clerk played by **Bryan Pringle**. Trumper died after falling downstairs in a pub when drunk, and Bryan Pringle enlisted all our sympathies for the sad man who kept to his own crooked principles when his master was losing his.

Trumper's funeral — one of those ornate send-offs, huge wreaths and all, which the crooked fraternity lay on for each other—was well observed and the final cops v. robbers chase to a background of plainsong was another unusual touch.

Coral Atkins as Shereen Anson, the imprisoned crook's flighty wife, played her raucous scenes with great gusto, and **Ronald Radd** pulled a splendid cameo out of the hat with his deadpan performance as Pigseyes, a millionaire.

This Way for Murder (RADIO)
A thriller in six parts: Part 3
By Victor Canning
Role - Unknown

"Raikes, planning a vast diamond haul for the Tintoc crime syndicate, is unaware that his assistant Sandra is reporting to the mysterious Pyramid organisation."
17/06/67

The Man in the Glass Booth. (THEATRE)
By Robert Shaw (Directed by Harold Pinter)
Role - Mrs Rosen

Harold Pinter's masterly direction, which evokes and points so many moods and feelings, sweeps through the evening. There is a brilliantly realised study of Goldman-Dorf by Donald Pleasence, whose biggest opportunity so far to show himself as an actor of real stature is taken superbly.

The others in the company have opportunities that amount to very much less, but making their particular mark are Sonia Dresdel, Yootha Joyce, Vernon Dobtcheff and Simon Kelly.

CAST
'THE MAN IN THE GLASS BOOTH'

Play by Robert Shaw. Presented by Peter Bridge, in assocation with Glasshouse Productions, at the St. Martin's on July 27. Designed by Voytek; lighting by Michael Northen; stage manager, Alan West.

Arthur Goldman	Donald Pleasence
Sam	Mark Heath
Jack	Simon Kelly
Charlie Cohn	Lawrence Pressman
Flower Man	Leon Lissek
Doctor Kessel	Terence Lodge
Rudin	Clifford Elkin
Mrs Rosen	Yootha Joyce
Steiger	Iain Blair
Durer	Mark Powell
Presiding Judge	Vernon Dobtcheff
Mrs Levi	Margaret Gibson
Old Man	Simon Kelly
Young man	Clifford Elkin
Solomon	Terence Lodge
Woman	Sonia Dresdel
Guards	Auton Low, Edwin Kuks

Directed by Harold Pinter

"Glynn and I lived very separate lives towards the end. - We slept in the same room but we had separate beds,. It was just one of those things, we loved one another very dearly, but we couldn't get on. - We were much happier when we were living together. As soon as we married, it was different. - There were fights between us as the hole in the ceiling testifies. - get me riled, get me angry, and they get it darling, wallop! It stops me getting high blood pressure or heart attacks – and let's face it they can always duck,- I can't remember what Glynn had said to me, but he went too far. I was cooking egg, bacon, sausages and chips at the time. I was so angry, I threw the lot at him, wham! Thank God the frying pan hit the ceiling darling. There was sizzling oil in it and I could have killed him - I have redecorated several times - but I shall never have the hole fixed. It reminds me not to throw things, I'm a chucker you see, I throw the first thing that comes to hand and I've always been a good shot." YOOTHA JOYCE

Work & Performance Highlights 1968

ITV Playhouse (TV)
"Your Name's Not God, It's Edgar"
Role 1. -Phoebe
Role 2. -Mrs. Bewley
By Jack Rosenthal

(On Alfred Lynch) *"Sometimes Alfred tells me I was awful when I think I have been rather good, which is a bit annoying, but mostly I think he is right."* YOOTHA JOYCE

A short thought turned into a long play

Jewel, doing splendidly his nasty old man, and **Yootha Joyce**, perfect as Phoebe, the fierce fiancée, completed the tight little triangle that imprisoned Edgar and forced him to repress all delicious thoughts of sex.

Finally, completely obsessed with the subject, he tore himself away to a dirty week-end in London with his mate Trev (**Richard Warwick**), made the landlady (Yootha Joyce again), and dashed back certain of finding Dad and Phoebe seriously injured as punishment for his wrongdoing. They weren't, but Edgar fell on to the railway line and broke three ribs. What the moral of that was I'm not sure.

Though fun was certainly to be had, and a great sense of the comic persisted to the end, there was no sign of structuring in the play. And oh my, an hour and a half of drama needs to be structured. It is no good meandering along from one funny scene to another—even if they are very funny scenes—without developing something, plot or theme or characters.

The plot here would have been used up nicely in a mid-morning story, the theme we knew about at once and there were no variations. The characters, though excellently played, even down to Blessed Art Thou (**Trevor Martin**), so called for his way among women, were little more than sketches accurately drawn for some more major work.

I hate to be ungrateful for a comedy play—they appear so seldom and when they are good they shine out like beacons in the darkness of second rate series and old films. Your Name's Not God, It's Edgar, was unfortunately not quite up to beacon standard and that was bal luck all round.

City 68' (TV)
"Love Thy Neighbour"
Role – Hilda

Height 5 feet 5 inches Gerry Cranham 1968

JOY JAMESON LTD
30, SLOANE STREET,
LONDON, S.W.1
TEL: 01-245 9551

YOOTHA JOYCE

Luther (TV)
By John Osborne
Role - Katharina Luther
"The man whose questioning was to shake the orthodox teachings of the Church and whose private agony was to threaten his own peace of mind"
21/12/68

Comedy Playhouse (TV)
Me Mammy (TV) (21 Episodes in total)
Pilot (Deleted)
By Hugh Leonard
"Bunjy is a top executive with a large firm in London. He is a bachelor with a luxury flat in Regent's Park, a sleek sports car —and all the freedom to indulge himself in glamorous sin. He is indeed the envy of all his married friends ...."
14/06/68

Nina Simone Live in England. (TV)
Yootha Joyce appears in audience of a concert. She is seated next to Cyril Smith.
Recorded for Granada TV in June 1968 (and broadcast on September 14). The special is titled Sound of Soul *and is divided into two halves. During the second half, Simone changed into an African robe and headdress.*
Nina Simone piano, vocal - Sam Waymon organ, vocal, percussion - Henry Young guitar - Gene Taylor bass - Buck Clarke drums.

Work & Performance Hghlights 1969

W. Somerset Maugham (TV)
"Lord Mountdrago"
Role – Elvira
22/07/69
"In his reply to a maiden speech of a Welsh M.P., Lord Mountdrago makes the man the laughing stock of Westminster and almost destroys his political career. Then for Mountdrago the repercussions begin. At night, in his dreams, he finds himself humiliated by the Welshman. When the dreams have parallels in reality he seeks the help of a psychiatrist, but Mountdrago is beyond help and he decides to take revenge in a bizarre and horrific way."

Armchair Theatre (TV)
"Go on... It'll Do You Good"
Role – Alice

> Jack Woolgar produced another rounded portrait in Mr. Higgs, the wily, rather grubby old man who twigged what was happening and defied all attempts to deal with him. **Barbara Couper**, a widow also marked down for disposal, gave a neat, crisp account of herself as Mrs. Tremlett.
>
> The sting in the tail came when Mr. Ledbetter's elderly mother (**Amy Dalby**), whom he had zealously protected from such expeditions, is whisked away under his nose.
>
> The whole idea an exaggeration? Yes, but it does not stretch the imagination too strenuously to imagine daughters like Mrs. Bulstrode (**Yootha Joyce**) and Mrs. Quartermain (**Pauline Yates**) weeping guilty crocodile tears all the way to the disposal centre in some future years when our senses have all been further hardened. The play parodied the heartlessness of bureaucracy and the whole edifice of State interference in people's lives. It was salutary—and fun.

ITV Sunday Night Theatre (TV)
"A Measure of Malice"
Role - Erica Seydoux

ITV's Sunday Night Theatre [TV series] as Erica Seydoux in **A Measure of Malice** *showed there were those who were well onto her abilities as an actress, stating "the cast gave the characters the depth they needed" "Yootha Joyce (what a pleasure to see this actress in a role worthy of her talent)."*

What impressed me most about this play was the writer's avoidance of the hackneyed cattiness with which someone less sensitive would have larded the dialogue. This was in-fighting with sheathed claws. Each woman was as sweet as honey to the other, and it was only by its effect on Lawrence that one could tell that a pitched battle was being fought, won and lost.

The cast gave the characters the depth they needed. Elizabeth Weather, kittenishly submissive but complacent at first, imperceptibly stripped away Eunice's veneer of self-assurance to show the frightened girl underneath.

John Stratton radiated the self-satisfaction of middle-aged affluence until Erica's influence waxed. Then the years fell away and Lawrence was young and foolish again. Yootha Joyce (what a pleasure to see this actress in a role worthy of her talent) left us in no doubt why Lawrence had once been so crazy about Erica, yet hinted at the regrets and insecurity that lay behind the woman's present air of self-confident vivacity.

This story of fleeting marital entanglement relied on characterisation, never plot. Indeed, the story could hardly have been simpler.

Eunice and Lawrence Kellers **Elizabeth Weather** and **John Stratton**) have a happy, prosperous marriage. Of the two, Lawrence seems the most rigidly bound to convention and the social virtues of punctuality and conformity. He is inclined to be pompous.

Into this cosy nest comes a cuckoo. Lawrence's one-time mistress Erica Seydouz (**Yootha Joyce**) has left her husband and is looking for somewhere to spend the night. Eunice persuades Lawrence to invite her to stay with them, smilingly admitting that she wants to "lay Erica's ghost".

The difference between the two women is immediately apparent. Erica appears feckless, disorganised, naively frank. Eunice damns her with faint praise, telling Lawrence that the older woman is like an endearing little girl.

Erica learns of this and gets her revenge. With shared reminiscences and old private jokes, she revives all Lawrence's youthful exuberance and sense of fun. Eunice becomes the odd woman out, a discomforted onlooker in her own home. Nostalgia acts as a powerful aphrodisiac and Lawrence willingly succumbs to Erica's provocative smiles.

Twenty Nine (TV)
Role - The Prostitute

BBC Play of the Month (TV)
"Maigret at Bay"
By Georges Simenon [Television play by Donald Bull]
Role - Mademoiselle Motte
09/02/69

Dixon of Dock Green (TV)
"Reluctant Witness"
By Gerard Kelsey
Role - Mrs. Harper
"Play with fire and you're liable to get burnt; play with crime and you're liable to get caught."
22/11/69

Me Mammy (TV)
Series 1, Episode 1 (Deleted)
"The Day We Blessed the Bench"
"Bunjy is torn between loyalties at home and at the office. Should he be at the blessing of the bench or at the opening of the new office wing?"
15/09/69

Standard Irish but it soon began to click

BY ANGELA MORETON

Me Mammy. BBC-1, September 8.

FOR the first ten minutes of Me Mammy my heart sank. Here were all the standard Irish jokes played out at full speed. Ageing lover boy, haridan mamma, rosaries, Holy Marys crossing oneself. Begorrah, we had the lot.

Then the playlet, the first of a series began to click. And ironically it really began to gather pace with the introduction of the heathen English so that it left one with the hope—and I think it is still no more than a hope—that the series will gel and provide something worthwhile.

The difficulty is to know how the writer can keep up the Irishisms. Good or bad they seemed to have been thrown in one a minute. "Praise the Lord", said Mammy, on receiving her horse winnings, "give me more winners". Or—"pray for the conversion of England". Or—"he thinks that sex is something Irishmen put potatoes in". There can't be all that many more of such witticisms and without them the playlets could subside like a deflated Irishman.

Perhaps more seriously, there look to be difficulties over the essential supporting roles. The erotic secretary-bird has been used; so, too, has the sensuous grass-widow next door. It is difficult to see how they can be incorporated further—which is a pity since **Yootha Joyce** as the one and **Diana Coupland** as the other made the most of their parts and brought a touch of reality to what had up to then been in danger of falling into the category of a period piece.

The trouble with plays about the Irish is that the characters are always played as feckless, lovable nuts. **Milo O'Shea** at least grasped the opportunity of the fat, flabby 40-year-old mother-dominated bachelor who has laid a trail around the office as something of a wild living boyo. But he spoiled some of the effect, at least, by rolling his eyes around, winking at the camera and giving a touch too much of hamming it up.

Anna Manahan as Mammy looked no older than Milo O'Shea so there was a feeling that she was completely underaged. She looked more like his cross sister than wild mamma.

Still—there was enough pace to make one feel that things were getting better as the play went along and it finished on a higher note than it started. I have reservations about the future course of the series, but enough interest to watch again to see whether I am right or wrong.

Me Mammy
Series 1, Episode 2 (deleted)
"The Day Verilia Went to Pieces"
"Bunjy is delighted that his mother and uncle, Fr Patrick, are going on a church outing-he hopes that he will have a quiet get-together with Miss Argyll during their absence ..."
22/09/69

Me Mammy
Series 1, Episode 3 (deleted)
"The Night Me Mammy Snuffed It"
"When his mother is taken off to hospital for observation, Bunjy hopes to make up for lost time with his girl friend. The Mammy, however, has made her own plans and these do not include Miss Argyll"
29/09/69

Me Mammy
Series 1, Episode 4 (deleted)
"The Day the Saints Went Marching Out"
"Bunjy buys his Mammy a plaster saint for a birthday present but her reaction to it is as unpredictable as ever"
13/10/69

Me Mammy
Series 1, Episode 5 (deleted)
"The First Time I Saw Paris"
"Bunjy is going to Paris on business with his secretary. His mother does not approve ..."
20/10/69

Me Mammy
Series 1, Episode 6 (deleted)
"The Day Concepta Got Engaged"
"Bunjy is in line for promotion and his boss decides to give a cocktail party for the short-listed applicants. And Mother came too ..."
27/10/69

Role - Miss Argyll

"I don't think Yootha had any dress-down clothes, but I wonder now what she wore when she walked her dogs?" **JOY JAMESON**

Work & Performance Hghlights 1970

Me Mammy (TV)
Series 2 Episodes (deleted)
- 07/08/70 The Night Miss Argyll Got Canonised
- 14/08/70 Me Mammys Tomb
- 21/08/70 The Night We Saw Old Nick
- 28/08/70 The Last of the Red Hot Mammies
- 04/09/70 The Night Edna Entered a Convent
- 11/09/70 The Night I Left the Church
- 18/09/70 The Morning After Finnegans Wake

Role - Miss Argyll

This was my first acquaintance with Bunjy Kennefick, his mother, and her efforts to keep her boy, forty if he's a day, from the temptations of the world.

The Irish whimsy and the wit and frankness of the Catholic humour were well to the fore in Hugh Leonard's splendid dialogue. This was well matched by the capable cast headed by Milo O'Shea, Anna Manahan, Yootha Joyce and David Kelly.

"It was at this point that things started to move for Yootha." GLYNN EDWARDS

"Most people see me as the funny tart, but I'm fairly good at being all wrought up and edgy, and the best thing I have done in ages was a middle-aged waitress with all kinds of problems. I've given more bad performances as an ordinary housewife than you've had hot dinners. I cannot see why I am offered those parts at all." YOOTHA JOYCE

"The trouble with **Me Mammy** *was that because I ran after a man in the programme, some people thought I was really like that. I had phone calls at home asking for dates. It got so bad at one time that I left the phone off the hook."*
YOOTHA JOYCE

To
The Rev. Frank Leshman.
With best wishes
from
"The Mamimg" Co.

and especially me,
Yootha Joyce.

Flat I,
198, Sussex Gdns,
London, W.2.
July 4th

Dear Rev. Lishman,

How lovely to hear from you! Sorry I haven't replied sooner — but, of course, your letter has travelled quite a lot. Finishing up in Spain! I went there for a few weeks, after the series finished, & only returned last week.

As you will now know, I hope, I relented towards dear Benjy at the last possible moment — and a lot of good it did me!

What a marvellous mix-up over Eileen Atkins! I shall tell her the story when next we meet. It will amuse her tremendously. Heaven knows — if you pardon me! — how it all happened.

Hope you don't mind — but I'm sending a little keepsake snap from us all. Father Patrick took it & Cousin Enda and The Mammy are helping to hold the likes straight! Sincere thanks.

Yootha Joyce.

"I have no idea what the allusion to me in the letter from Yootha is about! As far as I know, I never met Yootha Joyce, though of course I knew who she was. I have certainly never known a Reverend Lishman. I can only think that Yootha and I were mistaken for each other in some way, and in answering the Reverend's letter, Yootha pretended we were friends for some unknown reason." EILEEN ATKINS

The Misfit (TV)
"On Reading the Small Print"
Role – Pamela

Manhunt (TV)
"Fare Forward, Voyagers"
Role - Denise

Never Mind The Quality Feel The Width (FILM)
Role - Mrs Finch

Conceptions of Murder (TV)
"Peter and Maria"
Role - Maria Kurten

"I love to work and I am happy to play almost anything in television but my nerves about it are getting worse. What I really dread is having to pick up a cup and saucer in the first five minutes because it rattles so much." **YOOTHA JOYCE**

"Many, many times I've seen Yootha shaking with what I thought was nerves but may have been with drinking - but that's the chicken and the egg syndrome, isn't it? Did she drink because she needed it to settle her nerves? Maybe it usually does the trick. I can with my hand on my heart say I never knew Yootha had a drink problem. There was only ONE occasion...dinner at Mr. Chow's, Knightsbridge with Yootha, Basil, my husband, and me. In my mind I thought, God she can't half knock it back! That was because I'd never known anyone drink brandy all through the meal. Maybe three then wine. But Yootha was a smashing lady." **JOY JAMESON**

"Drinking? Well, Yootha was a very professional person, and I had these problems myself, especially when acting and a difficult bit comes up and you think you're going to dry up, but I wouldn't say she was a nervous performer." **GLYNN EDWARDS**

"If I had to stand in a witness box and swear how much Yootha drank, I would not be able to tell you. - There was never a time in my long association with Yootha that I was ever aware she was drunk." **BRIAN MURPHY**

Fragment of Fear (FILM)
Role - Miss Ward-Cadbury

"All kinds of people come up to you in shops or in the street and say, 'ooh you were lovely,' but quite often they don't know what you were lovely in." **YOOTHA JOYCE**

Yootha at Sandown Park 1970. Variety Club meeting.

Work & Performance Highlights 1971

Me Mammy (TV)
Series 3 Episodes
23/04/71 The Day We Went Dutch
30/04/71 The Night the Banshee Brought Me Home
07/05/71 The Day I Got Engaged
14/05/71 The Day I Went Commercial.
21/05/71 The Sacred Chemise of Miss Argyll.
28/05/71 The Mammy Murder Case
11/06/71 How To Be a Mammy In Law (Postponed from 4/6/71)

Role - Miss Argyll

The Victoria Line (RADIO)
"Liza Goddard and Yootha Joyce as Victoria and Edna say 'You want it, we find it' in the weekly adventures of an agency"
Episodes:
02/08/71
09/08/71
16/08/71
23/08/71
30/08/71
06/09/71
13/09/71
20/09/71

The Night Digger (FILM)
Role - Mrs. Palafox

All The Right Noises (FILM)
Role - Mrs. Bird – Landlady

" SHOW FOR VIETNAM," all proceeds of which will go to the Liberation Red Cross of South Vietnam and to the Vietnam Red Cross for use in North Vietnam, Laos and Cambodia, will take place, by permission of Sir Bernard Miles, at the Mermaid on Sunday, June 25 at 7.30 p.m. Artists appearing, subject to professional commitments, include Alfie Bass, Gaye Brown, Julie Felix, James Gibb, Jon Hendricks, Anthony Hopkins, Anne Jameson, Yootha Joyce, Bob Kerr's Whoopee Band, Malcolm McDowell, Joe Melia, George Melly, Adrian Mitchell, Brian Murphy, Richard O'Callaghan, Bryan Pringle, Annie Ross, Leon Rosselson, Janet Suzman and Gareth Thomas. The production has been organised by Peggy Kessell and Damon Sanders and is directed by Bill Owen, with readings arranged by R. D. Smith and an introduction written by James Cameron and spoken by Bill Owen.

Height 5 feet 5 inches   David Appleby 1971

JOY JAMESON LTD
7, WEST EATON PLACE MEWS
LONDON, SW1X 8LY
TEL 01-245 9551

YOOTHA JOYCE

"Yootha loved to be treated like a lady." "She loved having doors opened for her" **BRIAN MURPHY**

Work & Performance Highlights 1972

The Londoners. (THEATRE)
By Stephen Lewis
Role - Bridgie Judd

"Yootha was on board, playing Bridgie, a member of the Jugg family in **The Londoners**, *a reworking of* **Sparrers Can't Sing**. *She was joined by Rita Webb, Brian Murphy, Valerie Walsh, Bob Grant, and Ray Hoskins. The play had a new storyline, drawing on the far-reaching redevelopment of the Stratford East area, which was then a hot topic. The characters were shown coping with the demolition of their homes, and in their battles with the council planners".* **DEAR YOOTHA ... THE LIFE OF YOOTHA JOYCE**

"Miss Littlewood has done a superb job;- the characters were as real as your own neighbours." **THE TIMES**

"I liked the faithful-to-type performances of Yootha Joyce and Valerie Walsh" **THE EVENING NEWS**

"Yootha's performance was stimulating." **THE STAGE**

"Joan Littlewood told Yootha to play her character in **The Londoners** *(which led her and Brian Murphy to* **Man About The House**) *as a Cockney duchess."* **PETER RANKIN**

"Brian was a genius at improvisation and Yootha was a genius at responding to it. I'm using that silly word genius, but you know what I mean!" **DUDLEY SUTTON**

The imaginative and adroit John Littlewood is clearly at work, but I felt disappointed to find nothing new in production, message or material.

Rita Webb now plays Grannie Miggs, a part created wonderfully by Amelia Bayntun. Miss Webb brings her own conviction to the character, but it is a pale reminder of the memorable original. There are brilliant performances, fine in themselves as they perfectly blend with the production, by Stephen Lewis, Bob Grant and Brian Murphy, and the entertainment is further stimulated by Ron Hackett, Yootha Joyce and Bob Kerr's Whoopee Band.

Tales From The Lazy Acre (TV)
"The Last Great Pint-Drinking Tournament"
Role - Mrs Gaynor (English Landlady)
08/05/72

The production was well mounted and presented with a style that began to grow on one. What particularly impressed me was the beautifully filmed opening and closing sequences. They, in themselves, were an incentive to visit Dublin's Lazy Acre which would, I am sure, make one more appreciative of its humour.

Mossy Noonan (Milo O'Shea), who was persuaded to enter a beer-drinking competition by a representative of the Devil, a solicitor who could well have come from Hammer House as could his attractive fang-toothed assistant.

In addition to receiving a silver cup the winner was also entitled to the favours of the English landlady, the suitably blonde and brassy Mrs Gaynor (Yootha Joyce) but, as alcohol had always taken its toll this prize had never been claimed. However, there is always a first

Afternoon Theatre (RADIO)
"The Truth Game"
By Derek Hoddinott
Role – Unknown

"Yootha Joyce and Sheila Grant ' I've got a nice bank account, a pleasant flat - sports car. holidays abroad. It's the " I'm all right Jack" syndrome. Open the door and join the club Neil! You can' run with the hare and hunt with the hounds. Not on this one!"
05/08/72

Steptoe and Son (RADIO)
"The Bonds That Bind Us"
Role – Girlfriend
02/09/72

"Actor Ian Burford, who worked alongside Yootha in a radio recording of 'The Bonds That Bind Us,' an episode of Steptoe and Son, remembered that the producer, "who was also the warm-up man, introduced her to the audience in a less than subtle way, 'well Yootha Joyce, what can I say.... Whaaaaarrr!' Yootha was less than pleased and entered through the curtains to face the audience with a face like thunder. I'm sure that in such circumstances Yootha was not a person to hide her feelings." DEAR YOOTHA… THE LIFE OF YOOTHA JOYCE

Everyone was a little bit, er, careful when they were discussing something with Yootha, - she had big blue eyes, and if you got a gaze out of them, they could turn black, if she was not well pleased!" "At your own peril did you get the wrong side of Yootha!" PETER FRAZER JONES

Tarbuck's Luck (TV)
Role – Unknown
15/04/72

8.30 pm *Colour*
Tarbuck's Luck
Written by
MIKE CRAIG, LAWRIE KINSLEY
and RON MCDONNELL
starring
Jimmy Tarbuck
with his special guests
Patricia Hayes, Yootha Joyce
and Vicky Leandros
with
FANNY CRADOCK, SHEILA O'NEILL

Jason King (TV)
"If It's Got to Go, It's Got to Go"
Role - Sister Dryker
"Yootha played alongside Peter Wyngarde in the title role, and Ivor Salter, her colleague from repertory days, who played Lorik"

Nearest and Dearest (FILM)
Role - Mrs. Rhoda Rowbottom

The Fenn Street Gang (TV)
"The Woman for Dennis"
Role – Glenda

Burke & Hare (FILM)
Role - Mrs. Hare

Body-snatching wife swappers are all just good friends

LESLIE WATKINS

WHICH wife is the real wife?

She's the blonde in the middle—getting the double-dose of cold shoulder.

For 26-year-old Christine Pilgrim has just been thrown into filmland's strangest matrimonial mix-up of the year.

And it's all because of her part in a film about the body-snatchers Burke and Hare.

That character canoodling on her right is her own real-life husband Glynn Edwards, who stars as Hare.

And the lady getting all his attention is 42-year-old Yootha Joyce, who plays his wife.

Clear so far? Well, hold on, this is where it gets involved. . . .

Yootha really WAS Glynn's wife. They were divorced about two years ago — then he married Christine.

On Christine's left is Derren Nesbitt, from ITV's "Special Branch," who stars as Burke. The girl in his arms, according to the script, is his wife—played by 28-year-old Dee S derey.

But, in real life, D Derren's cousin.

Like Derren said: " kept it all in the fam

So the only girl wi a husband is Christine real wife. She appears girl who "makes h useful" around a hou ill-repute.

"Yootha and I are chums," she said. " won't worry me whei has to share a bed wit husband."

Picture: TONY BA

"Yootha had extraordinary timing and could drop in a line, and land it faultlessly. Others would chase the laughs. Not her! She had them up her sleeve and slipped them in whenever there was a gap. And if there wasn't a gap, she waited until there was. - She also knew how to hold a moment on camera; I learned that from watching her during the filming of **Burke and Hare.**" CHRISTINE PILGRIM

"Yootha could make a dress from C&A look like a Dior or Chanel. She did shop at C&A sometimes actually. She never gave me fashion tips, just as she didn't give me acting ones. Although I remember discussing with her what we should wear to the wrap party for Burke and Hare *... or the premiere, I don't remember which. Anyway, I turned up in something lower cut and more diaphanous than we'd agreed, and she spat (though with a twinkle) 'Bitch!'"* **CHRISTINE PILGRIM**

DUNHILL INTERNATIONAL
SHOW JUMPING CHAMPIONSHIPS

GALA CHARITY PREMIERE

Dunhill International Show Jumping and the *National Society for Mentally Handicapped Children* would like to thank the following television companies and artists for their participation in the Charity Premiere at Olympia on Wednesday 19th December 1973

from

the BBC, **Barlow at Large** with Stratford Johns
the BBC, **Blue Peter** with Lesley Judd, John Noakes and Peter Purves
Granada TV, **Coronation Street** with Margot Bryant
ATV, **Crossroads** with Morris Parsons, Sonia Fox, Mona Ewins and Ann George
ATV, **General Hospital** with Jonathan Dennis, Carl Rigg, Monica Grey and Dudley Jones
Thames TV, **Man About The House** with Richard O'Sullivan, Paula Wilcox and Yootha Joyce

London Weekend, **Black Beauty** with Bill Lucas, Stacey Dorning, Charlotte Mitchell, Tony Maiden and Stephen Garlick
the BBC, **The Brothers** with Jean Anderson, Jennifer Wilson, Patrick O'Connell, Richard Easton, Hilary Tindall, Derek Benfield, Julia Goodman, Gillian McCutcheon and Anna Fox.
the BBC, **The Onedin Line** with Caroline Harris and Howard Lang
the BBC, **Z Cars** with Jimmy Ellis, John Slater, Ian Cullen and Douglas Fielding

and the artists who jumped in the N.S.M.H.C. Lufton Manor Stakes 'Black Beauty'
Brian Blessed
Suzanne Hall
Robert Hardy
Gerald Harper
Jimmy Hill
Christopher Neame
Douglas Raye
Mitzi Rogers

Work & Performance Highlights 1973

This Is Your Life (TV)
(George Sewell)
Role – Herself

Frankenstein: The True Story (TV)
Role - Hospital Matron; Mrs McGregor

Steptoe and Son Ride Again (FILM)
Role - Freda (Lennie's Wife)

On the Buses (TV)
"The Allowance"
Role – Jessie

7 of 1 (TV)
"Open All Hours"
Role - Mrs Scully

> Indeed it is a long time since I can recall a writer taking such a dominant hold of a situation comedy. For although there was little in the way of a plot there was always something worth listening to. That it came over so well reflects credit on a cast that included David Jason and Yootha Joyce, and on Sydney Lotterby's direction that captured the mood of the piece.

Comedy Playhouse (TV)
"Home from Home"
By Eric Davidson
Role - Lil Wilson
"Bill Collins may not have been the greatest husband of all time but when his wife moves into a bed-sitter and becomes a traffic warden - intent on making him her most frequent victim - things have gone too far."
08/02/73

Afternoon Theatre (RADIO)
"Comic's Code'
By Dominic Le Poer Power
"Good evening sir or madam. I represent the Nehemiah Bultitude Biblical Institute, and I am here to bring you the good news about the Nehemiah Illustrated Bible."
31/01/73

Man About the House (TV) (39 Episodes in total)
Series 1 Episodes
15/08/73   Three's a Crowd
22/08/73   And Mother Makes Four
29/08/73   Some Enchanted Evening
05/09/73   And Then There Were Two
12/09/73   It's Only Money
19/09/73   Match of the Day
26/09/73   No Children, No Dogs

25/12/73   Special Christmas Sketch: for ITV's **All Star Comedy Carnival** (1973)
Role - Mildred Roper

> As the caretaker's wife, who is not quite contented with the way her marriage is going, Yootha Joyce, is a super character. Miss Joyce is obviously going to have a big contribution to make to this show and I foresee some very funny situations, and this in itself is a mark of success because I am eagerly awaiting next week's episode to see what this team will get up to. Yootha is a delight and brings a character into the proceedings to contrast the youth element. It could all go their way but this superb characterisation is going to make a very strong mark. It has with me already.

"Our idea for a new sitcom, **Man About The House,** *came through reading the papers. In the small ads, we noticed that there were an increasing number of people advertising for 'mixed flat sharing' and as the subject hadn't been 'done,' we twisted it round a little, and made it two girls and one boy. Since the three kids sharing the flat had almost total freedom, with no parents to worry about, the downstairs landlord and landlady George and Mildred Roper became surrogate parents, authority figures."* **BRIAN COOKE**

"Brian phoned me up in great excitement one evening and said, 'I have been offered the most wonderful series about a man and a wife, it's a comedy.' I said 'how funny darling! I've been offered a series about an man and a wife' and he said, 'Let me know how you get on' and I said, 'fine.'" She also said: "the director knew him and the writers knew me! And of course it was the same series! When Brian phoned up he said, 'it's called **The Ropers.'** *I said, 'no it's not, it's called* **George and Mildred,'** *so I said 'oh, it's a different series,' then of course we got together eventually and found of course it was the same series, and we literally did not know that the other one had been cast opposite, they had just picked us out of a hat! It was like a raffle."* **YOOTHA JOYCE**

"We did some very funny scenes together, which was a great surprise to everyone, as the chemistry was already there. The others had to work harder to find and develop their characters but Yootha and I seemed to just drop in like old sinners." (…) *"even though we had our backs to one another, we sensed what we were going to do."* **BRIAN MURPHY**

Work & Performance Highlights 1974

Man About the House (FILM)
Role - Mildred Roper

"The film crew played a trick on us, replacing a picture prop of George and Mildred's wedding photograph with "this lovely picture of King Kong and a gorgon with lovely snakes coming out of its head. - That it really broke the ice and helped with the nerves. As it was a first scene, it took about thirty takes; we all fell about laughing so much, it was great fun." **YOOTHA JOYCE**

This Is Your Life (TV)
(Richard O'Sullivan)
Role – Herself

Man About The House (TV)
Series 2 Episodes
09/01/74   While the Cat's Away
16/01/74   Colour Me Yellow
23/01/74   In Praise of Older Men
30/01/74   Did You Ever Meet Rommel?
06/02/74   Two Foot Blue, Eyes of Blue
13/02/74   Carry Me Back to Old Southampton

Series 3 Episodes
09/10/74   Cuckoo in the Nest
16/10/74   Come into My Parlour
23/10/74   I Won't Dance, Don't Ask Me
30/10/74   Of Mice and Women
06/11/74   Somebody Out There Likes Me
13/11/74   We Shall Not Be Moved
20/11/74   Three of a Kind
Role - Mildred Roper

A NEW series of Thames's Man About The House will be starting transmission on October 9. Richard O'Sullivan, Paula Wilcox (right) and Sally Thomsett again star. Yootha Joyce and Brian Murphy play Mr and Mrs Roper, the couple from downstairs who own the house. Doug Fisher joins the cast for several of the episodes. Man About The House is written by Johnnie Mortimer and Brian Cooke and the series is produced and directed by Peter Frazer-Jones.

"You couldn't go through the door because someone had nailed it shut, so we had to come through the fireplace. The audience would love it when something went wrong." BRIAN MURPHY (on filming *George and Mildred*)

"Yootha was always friendly, and glamorous. - She would certainly scrub up well - We'd have rehearsals in our rehearsal room, for probably two and a half hours, then we'd all go to the pub over the road, or whatever pub was nearest, and stay there till God knows when, not late, but well into the afternoon and it was the same pattern for both **Man About The House** as the later *George and Mildred* series as well; it was very relaxed." PETER ERRINGTON (floor manager)

Admit One
Sunday, 11 July 1976   8.00 pm
Thames Television Studios
Teddington Lock
Teddington, Middlesex
Doors open 7.30 pm and close 7.45 pm

The after-show visits to the pub were obviously a great way for the cast and crew to relax after the rehearsals and recordings at the Thames Television Studios in Broom Road, Teddington. They certainly didn't draw any attention to the fact that Yootha was drinking too much alcohol. When I talked to Barbara Windsor, she told me that she "had heard of the rumours" of Yootha's drinking while working at Thames TV, when she was filming for the Carry On Christmas *TV specials. "Yootha was always professional, and I would only see her sipping the occasional glass of wine at intervals. But she clearly was a private drinker." The phrase is echoed by Yootha's solicitor Mario Uziell Hamilton, who, at Yootha's inquest, said that she "must have done her drinking secretly in her own home."* DEAR YOOTHA… THE LIFE OF YOOTHA JOYCE

Comedy Playhouse (TV)
"A Bird Alone"
By Hugh Leonard
Role - Unknown
02/04/74 (Recording date / Never Broadcast)

In **Our Betty - Scenes From My Life,** *her autobiography, Liz Smith says that the show was "never completed because it was considered 'too naughty.'" Liz played mother to Yootha Joyce's character. "It was beautifully written by Hugh Leonard, so you had wonderful real dialogue. Yootha's character was being divorced, with John Le Mesurier as the judge." In Liz's book she recalls, "The description I had to give to the judge of talking to Yootha behind the dress shop she owned while she was 'carrying on!,' was considered too shocking to go out." Very kindly, Liz Smith herself wrote to me recently about this show, which the BBC cancelled. She told me "It was a splendid show, a wonderful cast, wonderful writing and acting, just thrown away, and just look at the things they show today!""* DEAR YOOTHA… THE LIFE OF YOOTHA JOYCE

The Dick Emery Show (TV)
Series 4, Episode 12
Role – Vicar's Wife
29/10/74

"I had to change my phone number three times. I got really frightened when I went ex-directory and they still came through. When I phoned the police they said they couldn't act unless my life had been endangered. I changed the number again. I'm used to them now. It's a joke to me. If they breathe heavily, I just do the same. One bloke I upset rang again; to get my own back I blew a ship's foghorn down the line. He must have had earache for a week. Men like that don't worry me. Even if one had guts enough to stop me in the street, I could take care of myself." YOOTHA JOYCE

THOSE appearing in the benefit show at the Pindar of Wakefield, Gray's Inn Road, W.C.1, on February 23 include Kent Baker, Gaye Brown, Shaun Curry, Norma Dunbar, Yootha Joyce, Roy Kinnear, Brian Murphy, Bryan Pringle, Christine Pilgrim, Barrie Rutter, Christopher Sandford, Sheila Steafel, Peter Spraggon, Harry Towb and Bronwen Williams. It is organised by Aline Waites in aid of children suffering from spina bifida. Barry Cryer is in the chair and Barry Booth at the piano. The admission price is £3, with a reduction for Equity members.

Yootha snapped from above, Image Peter Roos.

Also past, but not forgotten — the efforts of all those personalities who assisted ALINE WAITES in her recent "ABA DABA MUSIC HALL" benefit show in aid of SPINAL BIFIDA children

Among those who kindly appeared at the PINDAR OF WAKEFIELD were GAYE BROWN, ROY KINNEAR, JO MELIA, BARRY CRYER, BARRY BOOTH, DAVID TATE, KENT BAKER, GEOFFREY ROBINSON, PETER SPRAGGON, HARRY TOWB, CHRISTOPHER SANDFORD, YOOTHA JOYCE, SHAUN CURRY, NORMA DUNBAR, BRIAN MURPHY, BRIAN PRINGLE, CHRISTINE PILGRIM, BARRY RUTTER, SHEILA STEAFEL, and

Yootha at a fancy dress party for the National Canine Defence League, dressed as Lillie Langtry.

"Yootha was a great champion for the cause, - our non-destruction policy was something that was very dear to her heart."
CLARISSA BALDWIN (Dogs' Trust)

I've always had pets, said Yootha, but it was quite accidental that I became involved with the NCDL. I always carry a spare lead with me so that I can take a stray dog in tow. Then they go to the League's kennels." "We [the League, that is] never put a healthy dog down - always find a home for it or else find someone to sponsor it, to pay for the League to keep it." She made it her business to promote the League's work; she appeared on radio to promote their good work as well as getting involved at the rescue centres herself. DEAR YOOTHA… THE LIFE OF YOOTHA JOYCE

"She was very supportive of charities and some of the entertainment industry charities in particular. - Whenever she would do her personal appearances for the animal charities, she had absolutely no sense of shame about persuading people to part with their money. Yootha would usually have the eyelashes go at full capacity and before you knew it you had your wallet out." **TERENCE LEE DICKSON**

Yootha canvassing for the NCDL.

Work & Performance Highlights 1975

Man About The House (TV)
Series 4 Episodes:
06/03/75   Home and Away
13/03/75   One for the Road
20/03/75   All in the Game
27/03/75   Never Give Your Real Name
03/04/75   The Tender Trap
10/04/75   My Son, My Son

Series 5 Episodes:
04/09/75   The Last Picture Show
11/09/75   Right Said George
18/09/75   A Little Knowledge
25/09/75   Love and Let Love
02/10/75   How Does Your Garden Grow?
09/10/75   Come Fly With Me
Role - Mildred Roper

"Her clothes that she wore as Mildred, well, the taste was not that different to her own: they were a cheap tacky version of the fairly outlandish clothes that she wore in real life." SALLY THOMSETT

Yootha Joyce and Brian Murphy, too, through "Man About The House" have established themselves as firm family favourites, and the roles they have created of "Mildred" and "George" have become house-hold names. Indeed, with the completion of the last "Man About The House" series, Thames TV are currently preparing a new situation comedy series based on the characters — simply called "George and Mildred" — for screening later this year.

"The two characters George and Mildred were becoming increasingly popular: Yootha recalled that the technicians on the studio floor would say: "'we hear you're going to have your own series', I'd say 'no darlings, not us'; and they were right, everybody knew it before Brian and me, we were the last to be told." DEAR YOOTHA... THE LIFE OF YOOTHA JOYCE

(Christmas) Celebrity Squares (TV)
Role – Herself
25/12/75

Password (RADIO)
Role – Herself
"*Esther Rantzcn , as chairwoman, helps contestants, who are partnered today by Yootha Joyce and Kenneth Williams*"
31/12/75

Boeing, Boeing. (THEATRE)
By Marc Camoletti [adapted by Beverly Cross]
Role - Bertha (The Maid)

"In early 1975, Yootha returned to the theatre to play Bertha, a maid, in Boeing, Boeing, *Marc Camoletti's French farce, adapted by Beverly Cross, which revolved around a Parisian bachelor and his numerous amours with airline stewardesses. She was joined by some of her* Man About the House *co-stars; Doug Fisher took the lead part of Bernard in the play, Richard O'Sullivan played Robert and Sally Thomsett, Judith. The play began a national tour in March and broke all box office records at the Wyvern theatre in Swindon. It went right round the country, and lasted for a number of months.* The Stage *said: "Yootha Joyce is superb as the maid. The timing and relative economy of her gestures contrast with the aimless arm waving of some of the other members of the cast. And these gestures and her expressions speak volumes of disapproval, resignation."* DEAR YOOTHA… THE LIFE OF YOOTHA JOYCE

CAMBRIDGE:
Arts. — "Boeing-Boeing," Richard O'Sullivan, Yootha Joyce, Sally Thomsett, Doug Fisher.

BOURNEMOUTH:
Pavilion. — Boeing-Boeing starring Richard O'Sullivan, Yootha Joyce, Sally Thomsett and Doug Fisher.

CARDIFF:
New. — "Boeing-Boeing" with Richard O'Sullivan, Yootha Joyce and Sally Thomsett.

BIRMINGHAM:
Alexandra. — "Boeing-Boeing," Richard O'Sullivan, Yootha Joyce, Sally Thomsett, Doug Fisher.

DUE to its success earlier this year, "Boeing-Boeing" starts another tour next Monday, September 22, with Richard O'Sullivan, Yootha Joyce, Sally Thomsett and Doug Fisher heading the cast, supported by Judy Matheson and Penelope Nice. The opening date is at Richmond Theatre, followed by Bath, Newcastle, Liverpool, Brighton, Bournemouth, Wolverhampton, Nottingham, Cardiff and Coventry. The play, written by Marc Camoletti and adapted from the French by Beverley Cross, is directed by Tony Clayton and designed by Royce Mills. Terry Lee Dickson is company manager. It is presented by Marilyn Davis and Royce Mills (for Mansion Plays Ltd) in association with Al Mitchell (for Noel Gay Artists). Press: Frank Rainbow, 734 1739.

THE WYVERN ARTS TRUST LTD.
congratulates

RICHARD O'SULLIVAN
Yootha Joyce, Sally Thomsett, Doug Fisher
Judy Matheson, Penelope Nice

on breaking all box office records with

BOEING - BOEING
at the Wyvern Theatre, Swindon
followed by a record breaking week at the
Alexandra Theatre, Birmingham
Directed by Tony Clayton. Designed by Royce Mills

A big thank you to Marilyn Davis and Al Mitchell and good luck for Leeds, Oxford, Cambridge, Wilmslow, Bradford, Edinburgh and Croydon.

THE entertainment value of the farce formula — irony, pretty girls and lots of doors — gets affirmation in the latest production of "Boeing Boeing," which made a very good start to a national tour at the Wyvern, Swindon, on March 10.

There is a point, early in the first act, when necessary explanations slow things down a bit, even in this slick production. But everything quickly revs up and faster flights produce mounting laughter.

Yootha Joyce is superb as the maid who suffers the farcical results of her employer's simultaneous engagement to three air-hostesses. The timing and relative economy of her gestures contrast with the aimless arm-waving of some of the other members of the cast. And these gestures and her expressions speak volumes of disapproval, surprise and a certain resignation — but even that has its breaking point, which comes inevitably as higher speed flying affects Bernard's ordered life.

Doug Fisher's performance reduces the suave, imperturbable young man of the opening scene to the dishevelled Bernard of the final curtain. He proves a good foil to Richard O'Sullivan's Robert, the naive lad from the provinces who undergoes quite a transformation when fast-thinking becomes essential.

Penelope Nice squeezes lots of comedy out of her caricature of the lively American gold-digger.

This production, directed by Tony Clayton, will be playing in about ten other regional theatres.
B.E.

"I have no grumbles and enjoy life. I have this nice flat, which I'm having modernised. I've even had the small yard landscaped. The gardeners were amused because it's only 30 feet by 12 feet, and they had never had to work with anything so small before. But they really put their hearts into it and have made it look beautiful." **YOOTHA JOYCE**

Yootha once confessed that she did have a tendency to "overdo the gold jewellery." She was often pictured wearing a Star of David bracelet and necklace; unfortunately I don't know what significance it had for her, if any; sadly nobody could tell me. As well as the jewellery, Yootha had "a love of expensive and beautifully cut clothes." One description of her appearance reported that "she flounced into her little London flat in a stunning, flowing pink number, 'like it darling? I think it's the sort of saucy thing George would like.'" **DEAR YOOTHA…THE LIFE OF YOOTHA JOYCE**

"I remember the ring on the left finger... great big knuckle duster... Ha! " **CHRISTINE PILGRIM**

She had not liked Terry (Lee Dickson) at the start; in the early stages of the tour of **Boeing Boeing**, *she admitted that she gradually came to admire him professionally, and before long Terry was "organising her personal life – with the title of personal manager, for his efforts." She said that "Good organisation" was something the "chaotic" Yootha has always been grateful for. Terry reinforced her "jaundiced view of self-imposed discipline."* **DEAR YOOTHA… THE LIFE OF YOOTHA JOYCE**

"The job of Stage Manager is to look after things technically and administratively, and for me, it was great touring, a different place each week. One of the things I would do is offer some kind of pastoral care to the company members, so before they left their homes, they had a full touring bible. They were told where the venue was, all the meeting times etc, and for **Boeing Boeing** *- for the whole 10 weeks. I would give them suggestions on places to stay, eat, schedules on getting from a to b, day by day information about press calls, local press interviews and so on.*
The cast, including Yootha, were kind of impressed with this. I think that 50% of other stage managers wouldn't dream of doing this sort of thing. They'd make their money, make the odd phone call and then bugger off home. I did this because I had worked with a lot of dancers who had expected this sort of thing. Dancers are very disciplined, and have very structured days and know exactly what they are doing with their detailed schedules, published usually 10 days ahead of schedule. So you see, I ran these schedules so that I knew where the buggers would be, and if anything went wrong, I knew I could find them and deal with them.
Now what used to happen with actors like Yootha is that they would usually, after a performance, just be left to their own resources, Now bear in mind Yootha was getting a lot attention from the public by playing Mildred Roper. I think Yootha found this organisation welcome." **TERENCE LEE DICKSON**

"Yootha loved her cuddly toys, she had quite a few, she had a Snoopy dog; she also had a Paddington bear. I also had a Paddington bear of my own, plus we both had a shared Paddington bear - this we both looked after." **TERENCE LEE DICKSON**

"There was a bunch of stuff that Yootha would get on with that was hers and a bunch of stuff that I would get on with that was mine." **TERENCE LEE DICKSON**

<u>Terence Lee Dickson – Brief biography</u>
"I was born in 1948 in London, and brought up in Mitcham. I attended a primary school in London in the Streatham area, and then the grammar school in Mitcham. From there I went to Central School of Speech and Drama, to do the stage management course, which in those days lasted two years. At the end of the first year, I decided I didn't really want to do the second half: they understood and found me a job across the road at Hampstead Theatre Club. From there I went and did repertory in Scotland, a year in Coventry, then went into the West End as a deputy stage manager. I worked abroad as a stage manager with a rather decent small-scale classical dance company.
I carried on in that right through the seventies, and became a general manager in the 1980's for a theatre company. I also went over to Canada for a while, then about 1989 I decided I'd had enough and set up a scenery production company in Battersea, which I did for many years, eventually relocating it to Kent. The company expanded into theming work for museums and attractions but continued making scenery mostly for theatre and television and for the past four or five years I have been trying to retire, but clients keep phoning up, wanting me to work for them. 90% of the work is overseas; mainly Europe, and it has been very successful."

"Yootha was perfectly good with a paintbrush, she was always quite practical. I remember we quite fancied barbequing things one time, so we went out in back garden and between us we built a brick barbeque. We did ordinary stuff that ordinary people do. I wasn't having a relationship with this famous woman on the television programme, I was having a relationship with a lady who lived in W2 and walked her dog in the park!" **TERENCE LEE DICKSON**

"I do try and give whatever I have to building a relationship, but I won't give more. In private life, I'm inclined to be extremely selfish. Anyone who's ever lived with me will tell you that.- When you're working, you go into a rehearsal room and say, 'My fellow's just left me' and they say, 'Darling, what a shame; now, about scene two.' No one tells you to have a good cry. Anyway, I'd hate to go in with red eyes, because I look awful with red eyes. - I never cried about Glynn or Cyril and I wouldn't cry about the next one. I've never cried in bed and I never will." YOOTHA JOYCE

"It was funny, In the series, Yootha was the strong, dominant type and I was the nervous one. But I don't really think that was the way things were in life. Yootha would be very honest with me, but I think we respected each other's private lives. She'd come up to me and say 'I've fallen in love again - isn't it silly?- We used to have so many rows in restaurants. There we'd be, shouting things like 'rubbish' and 'don't be stupid' at each other. She would have a go at me and I'd have a go back. Suddenly we'd fall about laughing. - We never, ever argued about the business - we were always in complete agreement about our work." BRIAN MURPHY

A snap shot of Yootha with Sammy (no head!) and the shop in Spain she claimed she was a "sleeping partner" in.

"I think there was a woman called Jenny that looked after the dog when Yootha went away. Jenny was a chum of Yootha's who herself had two Dutch barge dogs. Sammy the westie was a great walker; we had great times in the park with her down past the fountains and the gardens and all around the Serpentine in Hyde Park." TERENCE LEE DICKSON

"Yootha was a 'sleeping partner' with actress Christine Taylor and had a financial interest in **La Montañesa,** *in Monachil [in the Sierra Nevada]- an après ski shop specializing in sporting goods and souvenirs."*

Even in Spain, her concern for animals never left her: "when we go out there we feed the dogs and cats. About six in the evening a pack of dogs – virtually wild dogs – come round for all the scraps. Then about an hour later the cats come round. And I rescue donkeys too. The Spaniards think we're quite mad, but it's a question of conscience. I think anyone who throws a dog out of a car in this country is far more cruel than anything in Spain, because we are a society that supposedly respects animals." DEAR YOOTHA… THE LIFE OF YOOTHA JOYCE

She remembered sitting outside a cafe in Granada once, "when a busload of English ladies swamped me and I ran for my life – but that's the price you pay for being well known and being allowed into people's living rooms. It's very nice but it can be a bit too much at times, you feel trapped by the character people feel you are." DEAR YOOTHA… THE LIFE OF YOOTHA JOYCE

"My mother comes to Spain with me. I'm terrified of flying, so to keep my mind off it, we play cards all the time we're in the air. " YOOTHA JOYCE

"Yootha had an apartment in Nerja, Spain, which later changed hands: I don't know who took it, but she was very pleased to have it. - To help pay for its maintenance, it would be rented out in the high season; we both went there one Christmas and New Year and had a great time. When we went the following summer, it was let out, so we went to the Parador de Nerja instead, but at the apartment, there was a local guy there, an ex pat Brit. Not 100% happy with him – didn't like the shape of him at all. He behaved in a manner I would associate with someone pretending to be a retired army officer... I had no certain knowledge, but as far as I could tell, and going on what Yootha told me, there wasn't much left over from the rent money after his transgressions had been paid for! One of the reasons that she didn't go when she would have liked, was because she had so little spare time that it was unbelievable. Also, as she couldn't speak much Spanish, she spent a lot of time shopping, miming and drawing things instead. I remember one time she ran out of loo roll, and went to the local general store, in a town where you'd find two bars, a church with a priest that everybody hated, I think that was standard issue in Spain, I think if you enter the priesthood you never stay in the area that you were born and grew up in!
Anyway, Yootha entered this shop wanting the loo roll and she didn't know the words so attempted to mime it. The shopkeeper called his mother out and I think the whole village was coming into the shop to see what Yootha wanted. In the end, they dragged the priest out of the church, as he spoke some English. They were all disappointed that Yootha just wanted something so mundane, but even though it took about an hour and a half, she went out quite happily with her packet of loo rolls." TERENCE LEE DICKSON

The church in Frigiliana and one of her own snap shots of the stray cats she would feed in Spain.

"One of the problems with the flat near the coast in Spain was that it was starting to become more well known and she would feel more at home up at Frigiliana in the mountains; away from the crowds, because of course she would be mobbed. I would try and shield her a bit from it." TERENCE LEE DICKSON

"On the whole, my situation has been marvellously trouble-free. One's had one's despairing, despondent moments if work wasn't coming in. I used to think if I was out of work for three weeks I'd commit suicide. Now I can think of other things." YOOTHA JOYCE

"I really don't think she had a drinking problem until the last year of her life; we would drink white wine, sometimes with fizzy water, we would drink tea with lemon, but yeah, there was brandy about.
We had a Sunday lunch do which I catered for once, with a whole bunch of people from Thames Television appearing at the flat, I think we had just bought a video cassette recorder, and we bought a top end Bang and Olufsen hi fi system, for the occasion, which was actually quite disappointing. It wasn't anything like we were expecting, all face and no facility. We had Peter Frazer Jones, Brian Murphy and his wife Carol and a whole bunch of other people, about 10 I recall. I was pouring them all out some gin and tonics and Yootha came over and said, 'Don't give them all that to drink, they'll be falling over! You're giving them quadruples!' and of course, she gave me one of her looks, but it was all great fun. Interestingly though, there she was complaining that I was giving the guests too much to drink. Mind you, it was before dinner, and of course some of the guests were a touch pissed before the starters were on the table , so there was her attitude to drink."
"I tend to remember all the joy I had with Yootha; we had some brilliant times together."
TERENCE LEE DICKSON

"I've never wanted babies, never. It's not that I don't like children. I love children, providing they're other people's," she confessed. Joy Jameson confirmed that she "never thought Yootha was aching to have kids of her own." Yootha said, "My career had always come first. Besides, I know my limitations and I don't have the patience to cope with a baby and a career. Anyway I don't think I'd be a good mum. I'd be far too strict." It certainly wasn't that she was unable to have them: "I'm sure I could have had them like shelling peas." she once said, also saying she thought the whole thing was "slightly undignified." "Towards the end of our marriage we might have adopted one," she said, "but, as we were breaking up, it would have been very silly. I often wondered what would have happened if I'd had a child that was dull. I don't mind if they're not pretty, and if something was wrong, I'd love them to death, even more than if they were normal. But if they were dull, what would I do with them?" **DEAR YOOTHA…THE LIFE OF YOOTHA JOYCE**

"Being recognised on the street is a slight problem, but no one's knocking this" **YOOTHA JOYCE**

A charity event with Yootha and her mum (bottom)

"I was about 10. To be fair, I think she was getting fed up with lots of noisy cub scouts pushing and shoving to get her autograph. (The occasion was the 28th Shirley Cub Scout group setting the World Record for the longest line of coins in St George's Walk.)" stevek http://www.cpfc.org/forums/archive/index.php/t-154556-p-17.html

Work & Performance Highlights 1976

Man About The House (TV)
Series 6 Episodes
25/02/76   The Party's Over
03/03/76   One More for the Pot
10/03/76   The Generation Game
17/03/76   The Sunshine Boys
24/03/76   Mum Always Liked You Best
31/03/76   Fire Down Below
07/04/76   Another Bride Another Groom
Role - Mildred Roper

Whodunit? (TV)
"A Bad Habit"
Role - Herself

Looks Familiar (TV)
Role - Herself

The Wednesday Special: Pub Entertainer of the Year (TV)
Role - Herself (Judge)

THE PLAYBOYS

WINNERS OF THE PUB ENTERTAINER OF THE YEAR 1976

WINNERS OF TV TIMES TROPHY FOR ACT WITH GREATEST TV POTENTIAL

WOULD LIKE TO THANK THE CELEBRITIES (TITO BURNS, MERVYN CONN, NERYS HUGHES, MARTIN JACKSON, PETER JACKSON, JIMMY JEWEL, YOOTHA JOYCE, WILLIE RUSHTON, DENNIS WATERMAN and Chairman MIKE AIKEN) AND ALL CONCERNED FOR MAKING THEIR EVENING SUCH A MEMORABLE OCCASION.

AVAILABLE FOR CABARET WORK AND SUMMER SEASON 1977

ENQUIRIES: **DON PEARCE ENTERTAINMENTS LTD.**
DUCK LANE, MAIDS MORETON, BUCKINGHAM, BUCKS.
(02802) 2341/3909 (0908) 73242

● Panelists and VIPs at the Grosvenor Hotel's Great Room in Park Lane. Occasion was the Pub Entertainer of the Year final, won by THE PLAYBOYS who also received a cheque for £1000. Second was J. C. FIELD (£500) and third CANNED ROCK. The picture shows L to R MICHAEL AIKEN of St GEORGES TAVERNS, impresario TITO BURNS, TV columnist MARTIN JACKSON, impresario MERVYN CONN, JIMMY JEWEL, NERYS HUGHES, comedian FRANK CARSON, YOOTHA JOYCE, DENNIS WATERMAN.

Nobody Does It Like Marti [Caine] (TV)
Series 1, Episode 6
Role – Herself

The David Nixon Show (TV)
Series 7 Episode 5
Role - Herself

Those Wonderful TV Times (TV)
Series 3 Episode 1
Role – Herself

The TV Times Top Ten Awards (TV)
Role – Herself

SUN NEWSPAPER
Top television programme
  Starsky and Hutch (US series)
Top BBC series
  Starsky and Hutch
Top ITV series
  The Sweeney (Thames)
Top factual programme
  Sailor (BBC)
Top television personality
  Bruce Forsyth (BBC)
Top actor
  John Thaw (The Sweeney)
Top actress
  Yootha Joyce (George and Mildred, Thames)
Top comedy act
  The Two Ronnies (BBC)
Top children's personality
  Mike Reid (ITV)
Top sporting personality
  Dickie Davies (ITV)
Top pop group
  Abba

"I'm desperately imperious. I hate failure. One survives, but that isn't enough. You can survive in almost any way. I've never come to terms with failure and there's no way I'm going to change now. This is me, and if you don't like it, hard cheese." **YOOTHA JOYCE**

George & Mildred (TV) (38 Episodes in total)
Series 1 Episodes
06/09/76   Moving On
13/09/76   The Bad Penny
20/09/76   ... And Women Must Weep
27/09/76   Baby Talk
04/10/76   Your Money or Your Life
11/10/76   Where My Caravan Has Rested
18/10/76   The Little Dog Laughed
25/10/76   Best Foot Forward
01/11/76   My Husband Next Door
08/11/76   Family Planning
Role – Mildred Roper

"Yootha was very considerate to other actors. She was very generous to them; she would never crave for the funniest lines or anything like that. People would leave her stuff at the studios, gifts and things; she was well loved, and she was only ever in the studios for a day." **PETER ERRINGTON**

"We were close off-screen. Although we worked together a lot, we were never in each other's pockets." **BRIAN MURPHY**

Drawing by writer Brian Cooke.

"Mildred was great fun, and it was like, let's put the uniform on, with lots of negligees from Brentford Nylons because she used to like her nylon negligees, with lots of frills and things, and also bright colours, pink, and lime green. The earrings for the character were something we really went to town on; we would go out of our way to find the most outrageous and large baubles that you could find, which did catch the public's eye: very garish, but it was Mildred." **LYN HARVEY (COSTUME DESIGNER)**

"Yootha had great deal of tolerance of other people, she had a very sharp ability to evaluate someone's professional skills quite quickly."
"Yootha was skilful in the technical aspects of her job; she learned her lines easily, I know because I would read her lines with her. She would absorb direction rapidly, and with her you would get a very fast turnover at rehearsal." **TERENCE LEE DICKSON**

"All through our times together, we had a very good situation between the two of us on costs and money. We had a very straightforward deal; though a lot of people don't believe it, we went right down the middle. I was earning quite nicely, sometimes doing shows with Yootha, but most of the time I would be going off and doing other things. I remember she told me what she was getting for each episode of George and Mildred. *It was a big old number, but it wasn't that huge."*
TERENCE LEE DICKSON

Yootha Joyce's Mildred, lavishly adorned with synthetic leopard, was delicious, alternating between astringent contempt and wistful social aspiration.

it will take a riot squad to keep me away from Yootha Joyce and Brian Murphy's new comedy series, or Troy Kennedy Martin's opening script for The Sweeney.

YOOTHA JOYCE and BRIAN MURPHY play Mildred and George in what has become the most popular comedy show in the Jictar ratings Thames's George and Mildred.

"Yootha had very, very fine hair. She hated having it being dealt with by hairdressers. She would go to hairdressers, but it wasn't a pleasant day for her, so in fact, quite a lot, she would put a headscarf on rather than mess around with it. She wore wigs quite a lot too, not that it was thinning or anything like that, it was just a lot easier." **TERENCE LEE DICKSON**

Yootha herself spoke about playing the Mildred character "I hope to God I don't look anything like her off screen /stage – it's the wig that makes all the difference; anyone who looked like Mildred would be a disaster. She is a disaster, a very very sad little lady. She'd love to be like Ann, the posh lady next door. Sometimes she even buys the right dress, but she never can resist adding the plastic earrings and the whole bit. I glitter from ear to shoulder blades. All the jewellery gives her some kind of confidence, it's her front to the world. Mildred's a pathetic figure, most of all in the way she goes berserk over a little dog because she can't have a baby." DEAR YOOTHA… THE LIFE OF YOOTHA JOYCE

Nicholas Bond Owen told me that in George and Mildred, *Yootha was "definitely the star of the show." When I asked him what this "star" quality was, he told me: "Yootha always had a way of making everyone feel special, she had time for everyone and wasn't stuck up in any way whatsoever, she also had more lines and more costume changes than anyone else in the show and had to look the part in every scene, so she often had make up and wardrobe all over her on set, whereas the rest of us just turned up and said our lines! I also remember that we were often kept waiting for Yootha and she always made a grand entrance." DEAR YOOTHA… THE LIFE OF YOOTHA JOYCE*

"Yootha could really work a room; she had grace, she floated a little bit off the ground it seemed. – She would really like to wear clothes from one designer, usually from the prêt-à-porter range rather than the catwalk or couture range, and that designer was Yuki. These designs came in very sensuous fabrics and would be quite sculpted. Yootha's great figure became very sculptural in her presentation, swirling, boom! This, in contrast with Mildred Roper's look, which I often thought very angular, camp, almost like male drag, but then of course, she does have the gay following. The well known bold and unsubtle colours and prints of Mildred's outfits bore no relation to the clothes she wore for herself. If she wanted a posh frock it would have been vintage Schiaparelli." **TERENCE LEE DICKSON**

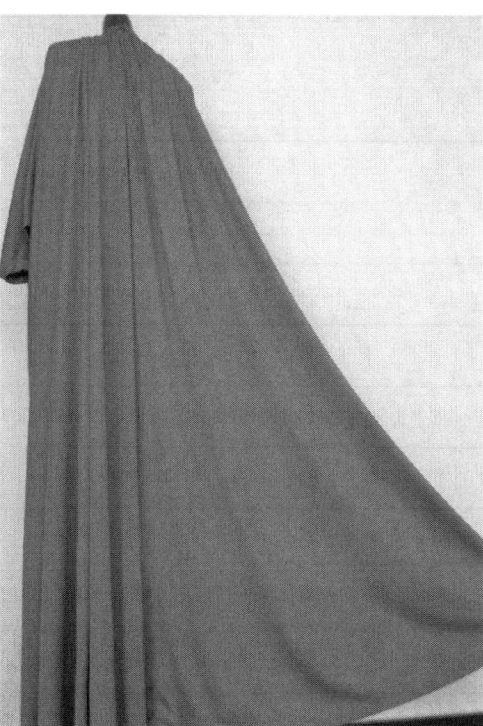

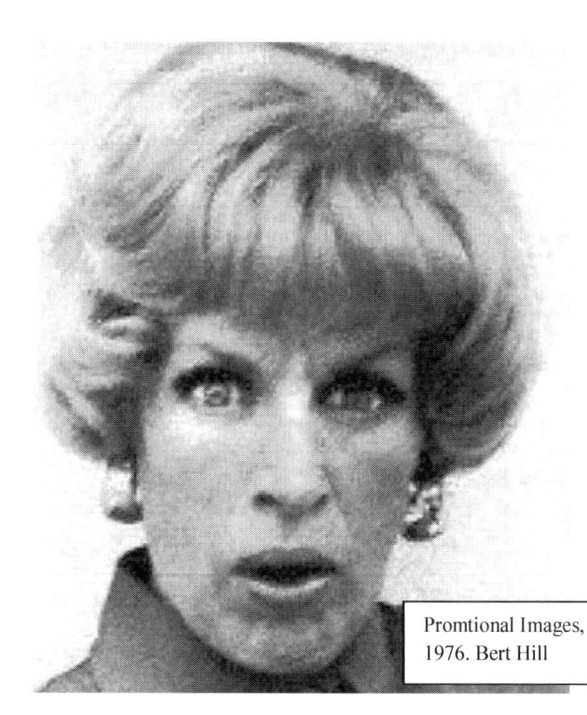

Promtional Images, 1976. Bert Hill

Cinderella. (THEATRE)
Adpt. Bryan Blackburn
Role - Mildred

Due to the record-breaking demand for tickets for the London PALLADIUM pantomime, CINDERELLA, which opened on Monday December 21, the run has been extended a further three weeks to 13 weeks.

It will now close on March 26.

Presented by LOUIS BENJAMIN and LESLIE GRADE, the pantomime stars RICHARD O'SULLIVAN as Buttons, YOOTHA JOYCE and BRIAN MURPHY as the Ugly Sisters and FIONA FULLERTON as Cinderella. Produced by ALBERT J. KNIGHT, it also stars ROGER DE COURCEY and NOOKIE, RICHARD (Mr. Pastry) HEARNE and singing star ROBERT YOUNG as Prince Charming.

The box office rush for Cinderella has followed a two-year absence of pantomime from the London Palladium — traditionally the home of Britain's Number 1 panto.

Produced by Jictar (Joint Industry Committee for Television Advertising Research) by AGB.

Monday, May 8 — Sunday, May 14

Network

		Individual viewing millions
1	European Cup Final: Liverpool v Bruges, ITV	19.20
2	George And Mildred, rpt, Thames	16.40
3	Armchair Thriller: The Limbo Connection, Tue, Thames	15.80
4	Coronation St, Wed, Granada	15.80
5	Winner Takes All, Yorkshire	15.60
6	Rising Damp, Yorkshire	15.10
7	Coronation St, Mon, Granada	14.55
7=	Armchair Thriller: The Limbo Connection, Thu, Thames	14.55
9	Crossroads, Fri, ATV	14.45
10	Celebrity Squares, ATV	14.20
11	Whodunnit?, Thames	14.10
12	Crossroads, Thu, ATV	14.05
13	Sale of the Century, Anglia	13.75
14	Get Some In!, Thames	13.15
14=	What's On Next?, Thames	13.15
16	Kojak (US), BBC	13.10
17	Crossroads, Tue, ATV	13.05
18	Home International Football: Wales v England, ITV	12.75
19	It's A Knockout, BBC	12.70
20	News At Ten, Wed, ITN	12.65

London

		TVR
1	Please Sir, film, ITV	32
2	Armchair Thriller: The Limbo Connection, Tue, Thames	31
3	Rising Damp, Yorkshire	30
3=	European Cup Final: Liverpool v Bruges, ITV	30
3=	Kojak (US), BBC	30
3=	That's Life, BBC	30
7	It's A Knockout, BBC	28
7=	The Val Doonican Music Show, BBC	28
9	George and Mildred, rpt, Thames	26
9=	Armchair Thriller: The Limbo Connection, Thu, Thames	26
9=	Two's Company, rpt, LWT	26

● Six of the star team who are bringing Pantomime back to London's West End this Christmas. Standing L to R: ALBERT J. KNIGHT (Producer), BRIAN MURPHY, RICHARD O'SULLIVAN. Seated, the ever more popular YOOTHA JOYCE between the presenters of 'CINDERELLA' at the PALLADIUM LOUIS BENJAMIN (R) & LESLIE GRADE.

"The press interest would get on Yootha's nerves more than mine. I knew what was going on, SHE knew what was going on - the rest of the world didn't, and the newspapers were making some standard assumptions. Looking back, I think she was more distressed than I was about them, the moral judgements from the press sold papers and made the news, which is what they wanted. In those days my policy was never to do any interviews with the press, but Yootha's friends knew that our relationship was proper and genuine. I remember Yootha's agent, Joy, a woman I had a lot of respect for. Joy had a house in Notting Hill next to a fabulous chippy, we would all go over and have fabulous fish and chips, we had lovely times."

"When we went out of course there were the usual blinding flashlights from the photographers, and it was all a bit strange at times, but then we would get back in the car and head back home, and we were just two folk who were together. One happened to be a wonderfully and immensely skilled actress, the other happened to be a reasonably well-known, pretty good stage manager. I think she recognised that as well as being good at what SHE did I was good at what I did."
TERENCE LEE DICKSON

Yootha spoke about her costumes, telling the punters that she was to wear the "highest heels possible" and as Brian "was in pumps," she could tower over him, bullying him as Georgina, much to the audience's delight. Joy Jameson remembers that Yootha was in her element there and "had a great time." The costumes themselves cost around £1,000 each, and were designed by Cynthia Tingey. Tingey's original pen, ink and gouache sketches were given to the Theatre Museum by her, and can be viewed online at the Victoria and Albert Museum's website, with a justly elaborate accompanying description. It is a shame there is no footage of the production. The reviews were good: Sidney Vauncez in The Stage *noted; "they all do extremely well, and the audience appear to enjoy every moment of it."* DEAR YOOTHA… THE LIFE OF YOOTHA JOYCE

Richard Hearne (Centre) with Yootha and Brian in Cinderella. 1976.

Tops of the bill are much-admired TV personalities, Richard O'Sullivan, from "Man About the House" and "Doctor at Large", as a smart, sophisticated but affable Buttons and Brian Murphy and Yootha Joyce of "George and Mildred" as the Ugly Sisters.

They all do extremely well and like the audience appear to enjoy every moment of it. Certainly Richard Hearne, the ageless "Mister Pastry", in the character of Baron Hardup, has the whale of a time amusing the kids while Nookie, the delightful cross-eyed little bear cheekily diverts the whole house regardless of age, squirming jauntily in the arms of his assistant Roger de Courcey, masquerading as a very personable Dandini.

Sidney Vauncez

"Yootha's mum was a lovely old stick. When Yootha was in panto at the Palladium – a show that went on for months and months – she actually came to stay with us in the flat in Paddington. We had a lovely Christmas I remember.
I would take Yootha to the Palladium for the first house, get her there for about 11.45, come back and look out for her mum. I checked she was all right and would take her out shopping locally. Then I would go back to the theatre between shows and see how Yootha was doing, then I'd whiz back to the flat, sit and talk to Maud for a bit, then go back for curtain down. They were doing three shows a day at the beginning of the season. That was six days a week and THAT was very tiring for Yootha.
In a way, in that stage show, the burden that she would have with the television show was now lifted a bit. That was because she had others in it like Richard O'Sullivan, Roger de Courcey, Fiona Fullerton and of course Richard Hearne, aka Mr. Pastry.
Yootha had seen Richard Hearne perform when she was a child and he was a big hit with her, playing Baron Hardup. I remember he did quite energetic dances, when, amazingly, this guy was in his 70s. There was a time, I recall, when

Yootha and Brian Murphy had found out the theatre management had ideas of cutting Hearne's part of the performance. Yootha got very upset about this and dragged Richard (O'Sullivan) and Brian (Murphy) along to see the manager and "had a word". She reminded him "who was doing what around here" and conveyed a "don't be a bloody fool" kind of attitude. I wasn't there but I heard about it, and the next thing we all knew is Mr. Pastry was up there doing the little dances as before. The proof they were right to object was the wonderful reaction from the auditorium. That was very pleasing for Yootha – she wasn't the type of person to put up with interference and stupidity from people."
"Yootha was mobbed everywhere she went. What we would do at theatres at the end of a show, where there would often be about 50 people outside of the stage door wanting autographs: we created a little booth with a window in the stage-doorkeeper's office, purely to keep everything safe and we would let in batches of six as Yootha really hated being mobbed."
TERENCE LEE DICKSON

Pete at the Palladium (RADIO)
"*Join Pete Murray at the London Palladium for his Christmas edition of Open House with his guests: Cilla Black, Jimmy Tarbuck, Richard O'Sullivan, Yootha Joyce. Brian Murphy and Gladys Mills*"
24/12/76

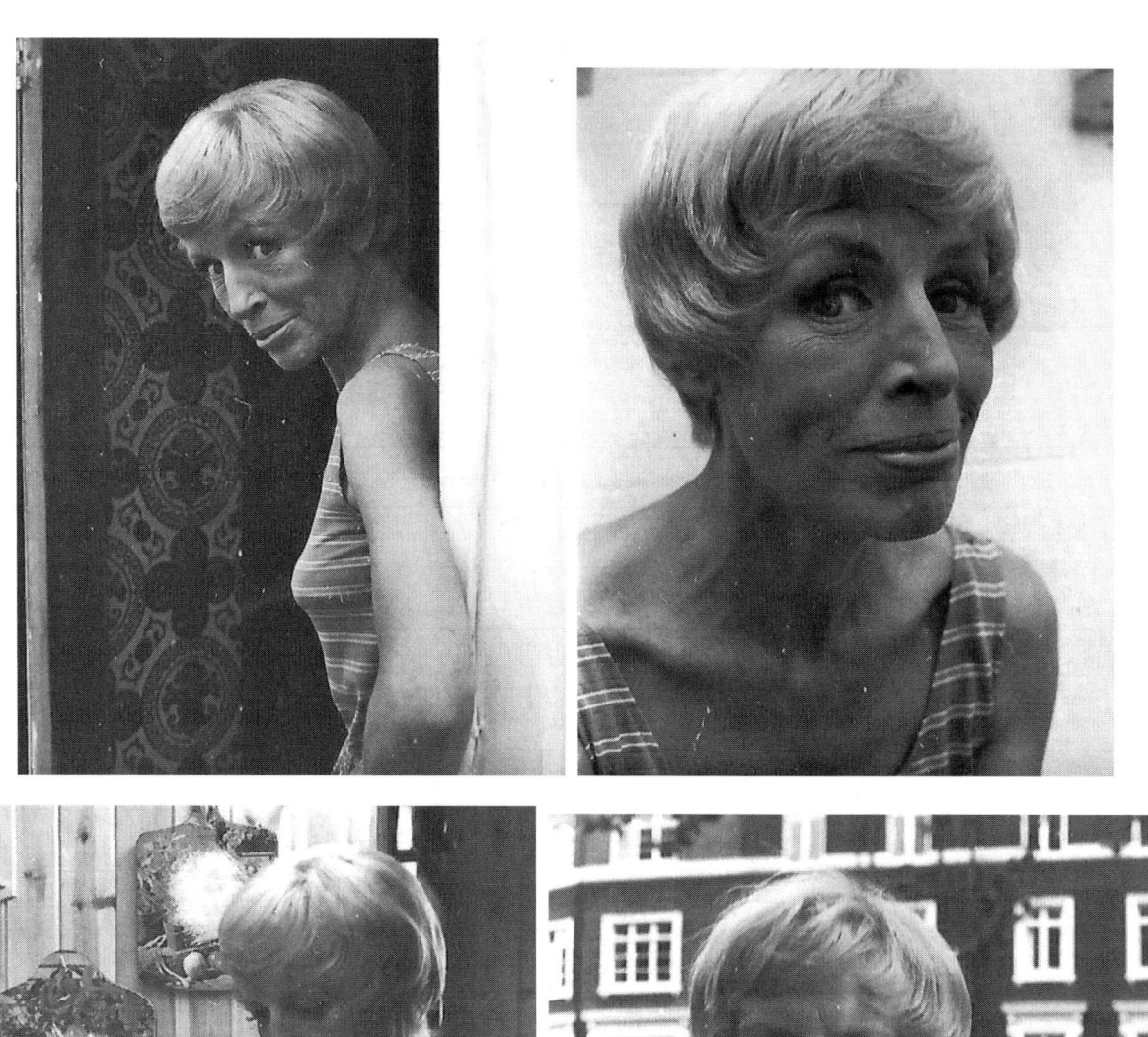

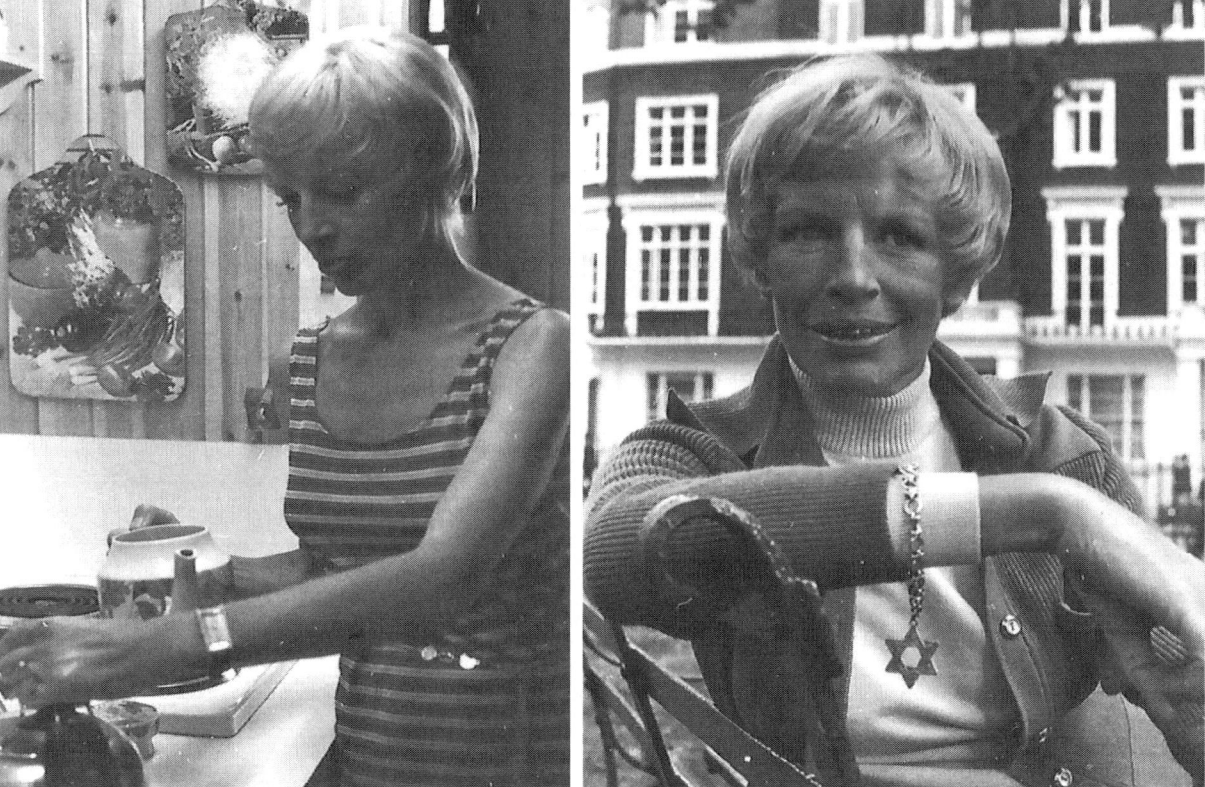

"Yootha frequently wore the Magen David which is the Hebrew for shield of David, (not the star of David, even though it does have the hexagram shape)" **TERENCE LEE DICKSON**

"The flat was always immaculate when I was there. Everything about Yootha was immaculate " **CHRISTINE PILGRIM**

Philip Jones, Controller of Light Entertainment, Thames Television, receives the CLUB MIRROR 'Special Award 1976' for his consistent and outstanding services to entertainment. In a friendly gesture his opposite number at BBC Television, BILL COTTON who won the Award last year, will present the Trophy and will no doubt have some flattering remarks to make about Philip Jones.

The presentation indicates that even rivals in this highly competitive field have a high regard for each other's talents.

Bob Potter, Proprietor of the Lakeside Club and highly respected in Clubland, receives the Club Mirror 'PERPETUAL CLUB OF THE YEAR" Award, a newly created accolade, in recognition of his outstanding achievements in the Club industry which gives Potter an unprecedented honour.

In creating this special Trophy the judges said: "His achievements have been so remarkable not only in 1976, but having won the 'Club of the Year' for two previous successive years we decided to give him an Award which will perpetuate his achievements for all time. It is a trophy he will retain."

He will receive the Trophy from a well known 'Surprise' star, whose identity will be a secret until the Award Evening.

Among the highlights of the Awards Evening are the Cavalcade of Stars and a Cabaret Tribute. Master magician DAVID NIXON will present the Cavalcade, introducing them in an exciting and novel way by creating a party atmosphere in

Work & Performance Highlights 1977

George & Mildred (TV)
Series 2 Episodes
14/11/77   Jumble Pie
21/11/77   All Around the Clock
28/11/77   The Travelling Man
05/12/77   The Unkindest Cut of All
12/12/77   The Right Way to Travel
19/12/77   The Dorothy Letters
26/12/77   No Business Like Show Business

Star Turn (TV)
"Bernard Cribbins invites George Chisholm, Yootha Joyce and Johnny Morris to compete with Windsor Davies, Barbara Windsor and Brian Cant in a series of peculiar acting games."
08/10/77

Pros and Cons (RADIO)
"An entertainment in which a series of confidence tricks are played before a panel of guest celebrities. They must decide who did what to whom - and how."
21/07/77

George & Mildred. (THEATRE)
UK Tour. By Johnnie Mortimer & Brian Cooke
Role - Mildred Roper

ALEXANDRA THEATRE - Birmingham

Director and Licensee: DEREK SALBERG   Administrator: MICHAEL BULLOCK

Week Comm. Mon. 13 June 1977

Monday to Friday 7.30 pm
Wednesday Matinee 2.30 pm
Saturday 5.0 pm & 8.0 pm

YOOTHA JOYCE   BRIAN MURPHY

in

The side-splitting new Comedy

GEORGE AND MILDRED

By JOHNNIE MORTIMER & BRIAN COOKE

Authors of T.V's 'MAN ABOUT THE HOUSE', 'ROBIN'S NEST' & 'GEORGE & MILDRED'

Prices: Stalls £1.75 £1.50 £1.00   Dress Circle £1.75 £1.50
Balcony £1.00 75p

Reduced prices (ex. Sats.) for Parties of 20 or more
Advance Booking Office: 10.00 a.m. to curtain rise 021-643-1231

Here the plays are presented annually by KIMBRELL-STEPHAM LTD, who this year have what must be the box office success certainty of all time — BRIAN MURPHY and YOOTHA JOYCE as GEORGE and MILDRED.

This is being presented with MARK FURNESS, and the comedy has been specially written for the summer season by JOHNNIE MORTIMER and BRIAN COOKE, who also wrote Man About the House and Robin's Nest.

George and Mildred will open at the ALEXANDRA THEATRE, Birmingham on June 13, play a week at the RICHMOND THEATRE, Richmond from June 20 and open a 16-week season at Bournemouth's Pier Theatre on June 27.

The same management are presenting a seven-week season of Caught on the Hop from May 9 with RICHARD EASTON, MARGARET ASHCROFT and DEREK BENFIELD, three stars from the television series, The Brothers.

PIER

Kimbrell-Stepham Associates and Mark Furness present GEORGE AND MILDRED with Yootha Joyce, Brian Murphy, Vanda Godsell, Peter Hughes, Sue Bond, Rosanne Wickes. Written by Johnnie Mortimer and Brian Cooke. Directed by Tony Clayton. Designed by Terry Parsons. (June 27 to October 15)

BOURNEMOUTH:

Pavilion. — The Val Doonican Show with Paul Daniels, Fiddlypig, Des Lane, Louisa Jane White and the Fred Peters Dancers

Pier Theatre. — George and Mildred with Yootha Joyce and Brian Murphy (Renee Stepham)

GEORGE AND MILDRED

Tailor-made to suit the television personalities created by BRIAN MURPHY and YOOTHA JOYCE, "George and Mildred", by JOHNNIE MORTIMER and BRIAN COOKE looks like being the most successful play ever presented in Bournemouth's PIER THEATRE.

Viewed purely as a play, it's a little thin in the story department and there are no prizes for guessing what happens next.

But with Brian and Yootha given superb material with which to snipe at each other continually, few give any thought to the plot but just sit back and rock with laughter.

Yootha Joyce has the best of the barbs, which she launches to poor Brian, constantly reminding him of his lack of prowess in the love stakes.

He defends himself as best he can, scoring points every now and again

● 'George and Mildred' join the James Boys fan Clubs.

● The JAMES BOYS, BRAD and STU, are fast becoming favourites among late-night audiences.
On their recent two appearances at THE IMPERIAL Nite Spot, Bournemouth, the act smashed all receipt records for the club, and have added many fans to their increasing popularity.
This breathtaking versatile young act work with the experience of veterans. They sing, dance, and play drums, clarinet and guitar with standards, Rock and Roll, songs of their own composition, and even a straw hat 'Good Old Days' routine.
Their musical rendition of 'Feelings' and 'Let There be drums' had the packed audiences to their feet with cries of more.
The room certainly had a mini Las Vegas look with their appearances with stars of the summer shows joining the acclaim among them YOOTHA JOYCE and BRIAN MURPHY, DAILEY and WAYNE, RODGER DE COURCEY, STU FRANCIS, MIKE ALEXANDRA (Peters and Lee, M.D.) SAMANTHA STEVENS DANCERS and NEW EDITION, and many more from the three summer shows.

BOURNEMOUTH PREMIER RESORT OF BRITAIN
LESLIE BERESFORD AND BOURNEMOUTH CORPORATION
WOULD LIKE TO SAY 'THANK YOU' TO

ROBERT LUFF
VAL DOONICAN
PAUL DANIELS
DES LANE
FIDDLYGIG
LOUISA JANE WHITE
FRED PETERS DANCERS
MORECAMBE AND WISE
ROLF HARRIS
LITTLE AND LARGE
NEW SEEKERS
THE BACHELORS
FRANKIE VAUGHAN
HINGE AND BRACKETT
DON WILLIAMS

M.A.M.'s
BARRY CLAYMAN & COLIN BERLIN
PETERS AND LEE
ROGER DE COURCEY & 'NOOKIE'
DAILEY AND WAYNE
STU FRANCIS
JODIE GREY
ROGER STEPHENSON & HIS PUPPETS
SAM'S SET
TOMMY COOPER
LESLIE CROWTHER
VINCE HILL
BERNI FLINT

KIMBRELL-STEPHAM ASSOCIATES
THE CAST OF 'GEORGE AND MILDRED'
YOOTHA JOYCE
BRIAN MURPHY
PETER HUGHES
VANDA GODSELL
ROSANNE WICKS and SUE BOND

JOHN HANSON
PAMELA FIELD
SOOTY & FRIENDS

THE CAST OF 'CAUGHT ON THE HOP'
MARGARET ASHCROFT
RICHARD EASTON
DEREK BENFIELD
PRIMI TOWNSEND
SHEILA COLLINGS
TREVOR GRIFFITHS
SALLY HARRISON
CLIFFORD EARL

FOR A MOST EXCITING SEASON

ALTHOUGH the hot summer of 1976 brought a drop in takings at two of Bournemouth's municipal theatres, the final accounts show a record net profit of nearly £271,000 for the catering and entertainments department.

The Freddie Starr Show at the Winter Gardens was the money spinner with box office receipts and the highest number of admission recorded since 1973, with an eventual net profit of £65,000. The Pier Theatre profit of £18,000 was £3,000 down on the previous year, but the committee expects a complete reversal this year with the booking of Yootha Joyce and Brian Murphy in "George and Mildred."

The Bachelors Show at the Pavilion improved the takings by £7,000, but attendances dropped by over 40,000. The Leslie Crowther pantomime at the same theatre was very successful with record box office receipts of £89,000.

Max Bygraves, Val Doonican, Yootha Joyce, Brian Murphy, Lennie Peters and Dianne Lee — that was the challenge thrown out by Bournemouth to every other resort in the country as it lined up its most star-studded summer season ever.

The result — packed theatres right from the early days of the summer shows, with July's heatwave making very little difference in some cases.

The big success story of the summer is George and Mildred at the Pier. For the first fortnight, there wasn't an empty seat second house and first houses were playing nightly to very respectably sized audiences.

There is no doubt that in George and Mildred, Brian Murphy and Yootha Joyce have created two of the best-loved television characters of all time.

Variety Club Dinner (Yootha far left)

TVTimes readers take their pick

THE results of TVTimes's annual readers' poll were announced last Thursday on the TVTimes Top Ten Awards Show on ITV, which was hosted by Richard O'Sullivan. Several performers retained the awards they won last year. They were Yootha Joyce, Bruce Forsyth and John Thaw as Jack Regan in The Sweeney.

The magazine instituted a new category of award this year — Television's Hall of Fame — for people making a long-standing contribution to television.

From the TVTimes 11 million readers, more than 60,000 voting coupons were received.

The awards went as follows:
Best actress — Gemma Jones
Best actor — Frank Finlay
Most compulsive male character — John Thaw as Jack Regan in Thames's The Sweeney
Most compulsive female character — Joanna Lumley as Purdey in The New Avengers
Funniest man — John Inman
Funniest woman — Yootha Joyce
Most popular male singer — David Soul
Most popular female singer — Julie Covington
Favourite male personality — Bruce Forsyth
Favourite female personality — Penelope Keith
Programme of the year — Granada's Disappearing World
Television's Hall of Fame award — Noele Gordon

MILDRED IN DOGHOUSE

Actress Yootha Joyce, star of the television series "George and Mildred," was in the doghouse yesterday — but she wasn't complaining.

She was visiting the Guildown Kennels at Froxfield, near Petersfield, which was recently taken over by the National Canine Defence League to care for abandoned dogs.

Hounded by cameramen, she was taking a break from performances at the Kings Theatre, Southsea, where she is appearing with Brian Murphy, who plays her husband George Roper in the stage version of the TV hit.

Christmas and New Year
Double Programmes Issue
14 Days of Glittering Entertainment on ITV
DECEMBER 24–JANUARY 6
TVTimes
Granada

Yootha at the Pier Theatre, Bournemouth taken by Tom Jones. . Image Courtesy Viv Jones.

Yootha at the Pier Theatre, Bournemouth, with Tom Jones (top left) and Viv Jones and her husband. Image Courtesy Viv Jones.

"Tom Jones; my dear brother, had great times with Yootha. Tom went to The Webber Douglas Academy where many famous actors attended, Terence Stamp, Donald Sinden, Hugh Bonneville, Anthony Sher to name but a few. He worked with Michael Gambon, Jonathan Pryce in the play 'Uncle Vanya'. He had a varied career in the theatre, also doing panto with Terry Scott and June Whitfield, Cannon and Ball and many more. Ironically he couldn't use his real name, as a certain singer had taken it! Even though Tom, the singer's real name was Woodward... Tom was trying to find a new surname and my hubby (knowing he had been reading Thomas Hardy novels) suggested Hardy! Now of course, there is another actor called Thomas Hardy! Tom also worked as a dresser for the greats, Morcambe and Wise and Benny Hill."

GRESHSTYLE PERSONAL APPEARANCES
AN ASSOCIATE COMPANY OF
CARL GRESHAM PROMOTIONS
IN ASSOCIATION WITH BARRY McMANUS
SUITE 7, THE TEXTILE HALL, ALDAMS ROAD, DEWSBURY WF12 8AE
TELEPHONES: DEWSBURY (STD. CODE: 0924) 468433/4 or 468686
FOR AND ON BEHALF OF

woolworth

The Precinct, COVENTRY, West Midlands
Telephones Coventry 22647 or 27446 Store Manager Mr. Graham Thomas
Issue this Autographed Greshprint of

YOOTHA JOYCE
(Co-Star of Thames TV Series 'George and Mildred')

Introduced by our compere Andy Hoffman

As a souvenir of the artiste's Personal appearance visit on Friday Morning, 19th November, 1976, at 10-30 a.m. to officially re-open their modernised Department store

Yootha Joyce was born in South London and attended Croydon High School. She trained at RADA and returned to Croydon to make her stage debut in "Escape me Never". This was followed by appearances at various Repertory Theatres. Under the direction of Joan Littlewood, Yootha spent five very rewarding years with the Theatre Workshop, and during these years she appeared in such productions as "The Hostage"; "Fings Ain't What They Used To Be" and "The Man in the Glass Booth". Her first Television credit came with "The Brothers in Law" and this was followed by numerous appearances in TV comedy series, including "Your Name's Not God"; "It's Edgar"; "A Measure of Malice"; "Lord Mountdrago"; "The Fenn Street Gang" and "On the Buses". On the cinema screen Yootha has made many appearances with more than a dozen full length feature films to her credit. Her highly successful role in "Man About the House" took her and her co-star Brian Murphy into their very own series. "George and Mildred", which took the viewers by storm and soon became the most popular programme on British Television. Towards the end of 1976 the Sun readers voted Yootha "Actress of the Year" and for the 1976/7 London Palladium pantomime both Yootha and Brian were booked to play "Ugly Sisters" in their production of "Cinderella". Yootha Joyce is today's real life Super Star — and a nice lady at that.

Yootha Joyce appears for Woolworth's by exclusive arrangement with Carl Gresham

This copyright handout was issued exclusively for our clients by GRESHSTYLE PHOTOPRINTS Limited, and must not be sold or reproduced in either part or whole under any circumstances whatever.

"Brian and his real wife Caroline knew Yootha for more than 20 years, from when they started work in the theatre. Later, when George and Mildred became successful, he and Yootha formed a special company.
"We called it BYROC, - The first two letters were for our Christian names, the second two for the Ropers, and the fifth was a C for Caroline, my wife."" BRIAN MURPHY

BYROC
PLAY PRODUCTIONS LTD.

DIRECTORS: YOOTHA JOYCE AND BRIAN MURPHY
168 SUSSEX GARDENS, W2

Mr. Alan Shepherd,
9, Finsbury Road,
Leicester.

21st January, 1977.

Dear Alan,

Thank you so much for your very nice letter.

I am so pleased that you enjoyed the series of 'George and Mildred' and thank you so much for taking the trouble to write and let me know.

I do hope that you enjoy the pantomime when you come along to see it.

I have great pleasure in enclosing an autographed photograph of myself.

With best wishes,

Yours sincerely,

Yootha Joyce

The Variety Club of Great Britain

Committee

TENT 36

Manchester Executive 1978

Chairman
JACK S. LEVY

Vice-Chairman
FRED SUMMERS

Treasurer
A. CHARLES DORNEY

Secretary
PETER R. ASH

Appeals Chairman
BARRY SPIERO

Publicity Officer
TOM TYRRELL

Past Chairmen
BERT RAPHAEL
COUNCILLOR FRED BALCOMBE J.P.
IVOR ROWE J.P.
ARTHUR SEARCH
KEITH WRIDE

Committee
MARTIN BURLIN
PETER DEARDEN
HAROLD FRANKS
ROY HALL
JIM HARVEY
DAVID MERCER
GRAHAM PYBUS
JOHN V.M. RUBIN
MONTY SAMUELS
ARTHUR W. WAINWRIGHT

celebrity luncheon

Hotel Piccadilly
Peacock Room
Thursday
26th January 1978

Handwritten inscriptions: "To Steven with lots of love Yootha Joyce (A WOMAN!) So Yours Momma Says!! xxx"

Yootha was very extravagant and generous with her gifts, Christine remembers. "They were always numerous, expensive and exquisitely wrapped." "One Christmas when my son Tom was a toddler, his gifts from Yootha included a toy garage and a Space 1999 Eagle Transporter spaceship. Tom remembers getting his head caught in the cat flap that Christmas. He had been out in Yootha's yard and tried to crawl back in through the cat flap." Both Christine and Tom agree that he doesn't seem to have been traumatised by the experience or to have a fetish about cat flaps! And he's a big noise in Corporate America these days so I'd say he came through it relatively unscathed," laughs Christine. DEAR YOOTHA… THE LIFE OF YOOTHA JOYCE

Investment Review
The Variety Club of Great Britain, Manchester

The Variety Club of Great Britain is an organisation whose sole aim is to render aid to children in need. This covers the entire spectrum of the handicapped, the orphaned, the hospitalised, the maladjusted and emotionally disturbed, the distressed, and those in any way deprived.

The Club is non-secretarian and non-political, and children of any religion, race or colour, and irrespective of background are eligible for help.

Although it raises an average of over £1m a year, the Club's administration costs are only 7 per cent—possibly the lowest deduction rate for overheads of any charity organisation in the country. One of the main reasons why it is possible to keep costs at a minimal level is because the bulk of the Club's work is administered personally by members, who donate also large contributions towards projects.

The Manchester Committee which was formed sixteen years ago has distributed over £500,000 in the Greater Manchester and Lancashire areas. They also have the largest Sunshine Coach fleet in the world, namely 192 coaches bringing happiness to tens of thousands of children every day.

In 1977, over £110,000 was distributed, five thousand toys, holidays for hundreds of children who never had the privilege of having one, help towards the building of holiday homes, and countless other appeals have been made.

The Committee had the privilege of hosting H.R.H. Princess Margaret and Earl Mountbatten of Burma, amongst the many highlights of the year's activities.

We look forward in 1978 to building a special Baby Dialysis Unit as one of our major projects, and to you all our supporters, our grateful thanks on behalf of all the children who have benefited from your abundant kindness.

MENU

Melon Honeydew

Roast Baby Chicken
Brussel Sprouts
Garden Peas
Roast Potatoes

Sherry Trifle

Coffee

"Give me the chance every serious minded actress jumps at, to expand and develop a character over a period of time, with the constant challenge of retaining audience interest, it really keeps you on your toes," **YOOTHA JOYCE**

Actor Robert Gillespie recalled "The director didn't see how petrified she was; she showed absolute terror. She came clean to me at the end of rehearsals saying, 'it doesn't get any better.' And she explained her fears to me. I was touched that this national star was talking to me openly about what a horrible task a live studio audience recording was, I was very moved to share those few moments with her." Even Brian Murphy recalled the moments of terror before a studio audience, "We used to wait backstage together before going on. We paced up and down the set prior to recording. I used to smoke then, and Yootha smoked like an old trooper. Despite our years of experience, it was still very nerve-wracking. We paced about so much that I swear we dug a trench in one of the studios with all our walking. She used to say to me, 'what are we doing this for, Brian?' I used to reply, 'er, money?,' and she said that was a good excuse, but once we were out there we did enjoy it." **DEAR YOOTHA… THE LIFE OF YOOTHA JOYCE**

"Yootha got nervous, but she didn't show it to me. I don't remember seeing her having more than a glass of wine before a performance. If she did drink any more, it must have been after she and I separated. But one thing that she may not have told other people was that when she was tiny, about 5 or 6, she had some difficulty sleeping. She told me that she remembers her dad, sometimes her mum, would give her a little glass of warm milk with some brandy in it, and this would send her off to sleep.
From my point of view, it is strange that the pair of them did that! Is that anything to do with the fact that she clearly had a drink or two? Or perhaps drink to excess at the end of her life – as has been reported to me, but remember, I never saw this! Maybe there's something in this; the habit for alcohol used for an awkward situation may just be locked in there, but I trained as a stage manager, not a psychologist, how the hell would I know?! The Yootha Joyce I knew was not a drunk. Her death was reported to have been cirrhosis of the liver, but moving things on a few decades, I guess her condition would have been dealt with by transplants, and these days frequently is." TERENCE LEE DICKSON

George and Mildred pop in for coffee

The entire cast of "George and Mildred," being staged at the Kings Theatre, Southsea, dropped in for coffee at New Park Road Community Centre, Chichester, yesterday.

They gave enthusiastic support for a fund-raising coffee morning and sale run by the Chichester Friends of the Home Farm Trust.

The Trust sets up working homes for mentally handicapped young adults, and the Chichester Friends are hoping to inspire enthusiasm and cash for a home in Sussex.

Yootha Joyce, Brian Murphy, Reginald Marsh, Dylis Laye, Sue Bond, and Katie Fawkes brought many gifts for the sale and were kept busy signing autographs for their fans. Brian also played an active part by auctioning various items.

"We are wholeheartedly behind the Trust and hope that many people will realize what a worthwhile appeal this is," said Brian.

The whole cast were delighted with the response to the Southsea show, which was playing to packed houses. "They have even opened the balcony to fit more people in," he said.

"There were three places she would go for shopping and they were places which were just round the corner from her flat, Marks and Spencer's was one, and more importantly shopkeepers knew her, so if she ever got any interruptions or hassle, the shopkeepers would usually help her out." TERENCE LEE DICKSON

The White Elephant on the River as it was recently. It has since been demolished.

"She loved her brandy. And no one would dare suggest she cut back on it – not her mother, Glynn and certainly not me. I remember her once getting short with her mother – a delightful, mild, caring lady, when she ordered steak tartare, on my recommendation (gulp!), at the White Elephant on the River, "Mother," she said, "It's raw steak and raw egg! Do you think you're going to be able to eat that? Don't be ridiculous!"

"Can you imagine her mother daring to tell her to stop drinking?! - I'd say that Yootha suffered quite a lot regarding whether or not she was wanted... although to see her with her mum... you'd not think so. Her mother seemed to dote on her... to the point that she was a wee bit intimidated by her." CHRISTINE PILGRIM

Asking Glynn Edwards whether Yootha's performance met with her mother's approval, he told me it did, "and with the sitcom's success after success, Maud was very proud of that." DEAR YOOTHA… THE LIFE OF YOOTHA JOYCE

"The White Elephant on the River has been demolished and replaced with high priced flats. - The Ellie on the River was a venture owned and operated by the same guy as had the White Elephant, which was a members' club in Curzon Street. The last time I, was at the River one was for the opening night party for Fiddler On The Roof *at the Apollo Victoria (then the New Victoria Theatre) in the early 80s. It was still a members' club then and reasonably priced. The kitchen always operated until quite late and there was a large dance floor and a good band. Another place we liked was Macready's in Covent Garden, again a private club offering late kitchen, reasonable prices and some relief from the public gaze.*
TERENCE LEE DICKSON

on Saturday nights. When cabaret acts are on stage, bingo will stop.

The first star booked is Yootha Joyce, of "George and Mildred" fame, who will perform the official opening ceremony of the club on Thursday, October 19. Also scheduled to appear at the Beacon in October are Kenny Lynch on the 21st and Pat Phoenix the following Saturday. November and December bookings have not yet been finalised.

The Beacon is an ambitious venture with two licensed bars, a restaurant in the club foyer, a full waitress service for drinks, a whole range of food from grills to basket meals and ample car-parking facilities. £18,000 has been spent on wall-to-wall carpeting alone. Manager Alan King will act as compere.

"What Yootha ordered at a restaurant, depended on the time of day – she didn't like to eat before performances, even during rehearsals! After a studio recording we would all zip off to a particular Italian restaurant in Teddington. Yootha would order insalata tricolore to start with. A main course would probably be pan fried liver with some sauté potatoes, with salad or vegetables on the side. If we were at the White Elephant on the River, it may be chopped liver starter, a typical main would be veal escalopes – red veal was preferable, not white: she was quite picky about things like that. Her appetite, I remember, was relatively small." TERENCE LEE DICKSON

Work & Performance Highlights 1978

George & Mildred (TV)
Series 3, Episodes
07/09/78   Opportunity Knocks
14/09/78   And So to Bed
21/09/78   I Believe in Yesterday
28/09/78   The Four Letter Word
05/10/78   The Delivery Man
12/10/78   Life with Father

Series 4, Episodes
16/11/78   Just the Job
23/11/78   Days of Beer and Rosie
30/11/78   You Must Have Showers
07/12/78   All Work and No Pay
14/12/78   Nappy Days
21/12/78   The Mating Game
27/12/78   On the Second Day of Christmas
Role -- Mildred Roper

George & Mildred. (THEATRE)
UK Tour. By Johnnie Mortimer & Brian Cooke
Role - Mildred Roper

WORK is expected to start on Bournemouth's new show place on the Pier in October 1979. Early plans show that the upper floor will have a show bar, stage and dressing rooms, at ground floor level will be an amusement area, five shops, staff workshops, box office and toilets. At beach level there will be a safety boat store and other storage areas.

The pier will still remain open to the public during reconstruction which is expected to take two years and will cost in the region of £800,000. Profits last year, when the play "George & Mildred" played the summer season there with Yootha Joyce and Brian Murphy topped a record £62,000.

Writer of the best female role created for television: Johnny Mortimer and Brian Cooke for Mildred in Thames's George and Mildred. An award also went to Yootha Joyce who plays the part of Mildred.

NOTTINGHAM:
Theatre Royal (Moss). — George and Mildred — Yootha Joyce, Brian Murphy, Reginald Marsh, Dilys Laye (Renee Stepham).

Grand. — George & Mildred. — Yootha Joyce, Brian Murphy, Reginald Marsh, Dilys Laye (Renee Stepham).

GLASGOW:
King's. — George and Mildred. — Yootha Joyce, Brian Murphy, Reginald Marsh, Dilys Laye (Renee Stephan).

STEPHAM-BELL PROMOTIONS LTD.
and
MARK FURNESS
(for Barbara Plays Ltd)
present

'GEORGE AND MILDRED'

JERSEY
Opera House — George and Mildred — Yootha Joyce, Brian Murphy, Dilys Laye, Reginald Marsh (Stepham).

Lesley Dail, Trevor Jones.
SOUTHSEA:
King's. — George and Mildred — Yootha Joyce, Brian Murphy, Dilys Laye, Reginald Marsh.
SWINDON

The *George and Mildred* tour stage set.

The other side

When one hears how television is reputed to have been responsible for the decline of the theatre, particularly in the provinces, it is worth remembering that there is another side to the coin.

Yootha Joyce and Brian Murphy are currently touring in Johnnie Mortimer and Brian Cooke's farce George and Mildred which is, of course, based on the popular Thames series of the same name. They are attracting capacity houses, while the gross take at the Leeds Grand topped £20,000 — a record for the theatre.

"I remember Yootha being a bit concerned working in Jersey on the George and Mildred *stage show. She was booked to do quite a lengthy season at St Helier. She wanted me to be there just to look after everything. Yootha's mum had not been well at all in the year before. It was just after a big old thrash for Maud's birthday party. During the meal Maud had felt unwell; she went upstairs to rest and next thing was they called an ambulance. Maud had to go into hospital for a while. I think she may have had a mild heart attack."* TERENCE LEE DICKSON

'George and Mildred' — the Opera House presents a winner

TONY WEBSTER reports

ON television, it's Yootha Joyce's "Mildred" which comes out tops in the laughter stakes, but at the Opera House, Brian Roper's "George" comes across loud and clear as an equal situation comedy bill-topper.

The two characters, who were created in "Man About the House", play to perfection on stage the rôles which have kept "George and Mildred" at the top of television ratings, with the applause which accompanied the final curtain at yesterday's first night proving that they will be top of everyone's entertainment tree in Jersey this summer.

The elegantly-dressed Mildred and the shabby George, complete with carpet slippers on occasions, make the perfect comedy couple, and when they are backed-up on stage by two other talented people — Dilys Laye and Reginald Marsh — the result is two hours of sheer hilarity.

Much of the stage version of "George and Mildred" is pure farce, but then so is the television series, of which I admit to not being too big a fan.

But on stage, they're magic. The play is well rehearsed, everyone is perfect for their rôles, and there's a neat comedy twist at the end.

The story begins with George refusing to go on a second honeymoon with Mildred, and when her sister, Ethel (Dilys), leaves hubby Humphrey (Reginald), the two sisters decide to go away on their own.

Ethel is positive that Humphrey has been playing around with his secretary, Jennifer (Sue Bond), and the audience soon discovers that she is right when, soon after the wives' departure for France, he makes a date for a meal with that secretary.

But he has got this friend, Shirley (Susanna Pope), and won't go without her. So guess who makes up a foursome? That's right, good old George.

After the meal, all four go back to the Roper's house for a party, and this is where the farce really begins, because while the girls are in the bathroom who should walk out of the bedroom but Mildred and Ethel...

Trousers are dropped, sexy underwear is on display, the "nudge nudge, wink wink" jokes abound, and all in all, great hilarity is in abundance.

I particularly remember George for the way in which he zooms across the room when not sitting in bed eating a cream cracker and a pickled onion, while Mildred's portrayal of a frustrated wife seems to be perfect.

She and George are perfect foils for each other, with Ethel also doing her part when George puts across one of his jokes.

Ethel is quite snobbish, you see, and when Mildred asks if her dress is new, Ethel replies: "Yes, it's one of Pierre Gardin's."

Enter George: "Oh, he's the same size as you, is he?"

The result is laughter from everyone — and that's only one gem from a comedy play packed with them as richly as a diamond mine.

The action takes place over two weekends, and only one set is used, the very modern living room of Ropers' house in Hampton Wick.

Written by Johnnie Mortimer and Brian Cooke, "George and Mildred", is directed by Tony Clayton and designed by Terry Parsons. It is presented by Dick Ray.

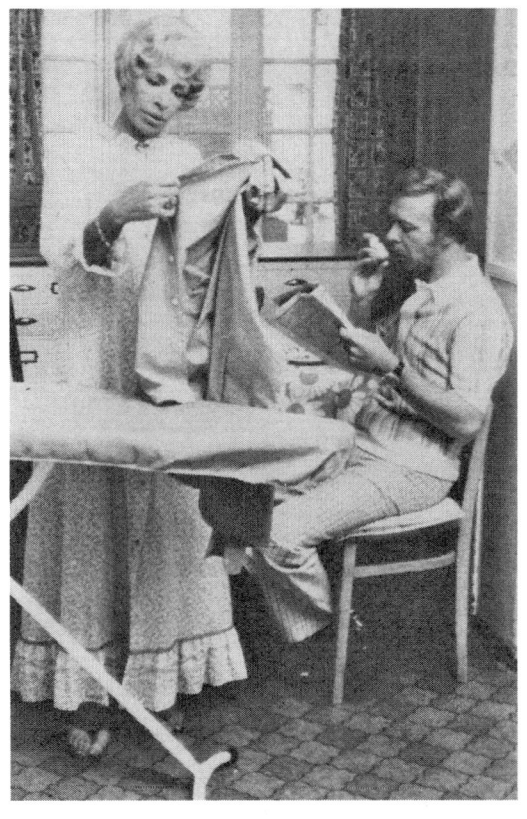

"I should like to say goodbye to them by the end of 1979, and so would Brian. It will take us at least a year to get rid of the image; the repeats will always be around. If we go on for very much longer we will never do anything except be George and Mildred, it's flattering, it's security, it's profitable – but it isn't good for an actor or actress, and that matters to us, desperately." YOOTHA JOYCE

"Yootha basically played Yootha, I suppose. I mean she did act but she smoked, she drank, she did all that as the character, as she did in life and it sort of transferred on screen." PETER ERRINGTON

Sally Thomsett said that Yootha, arguably, was like Mildred, "a very flirty lady. She came across as this big fierce domineering masculine person, but she wasn't, she was very feminine and very flirtatious." DEAR YOOTHA… THE LIFE OF YOOTHA JOYCE

International appreciation of Yootha's work was also noted as far way as Australia. The Canberra Times *thought she had great abilities as an actress in the show as Mildred, "She brought the character to life with her ability to draw the maximum amount of vinegar from an acid line." DEAR YOOTHA… THE LIFE OF YOOTHA JOYCE*

RENEE STEPHAM would like to thank

Pier Theatre
BOURNEMOUTH
Leslie Beresford (Kimbrell-Stepham Associates with Mark Furness)

"GEORGE AND MILDRED"
Yootha Joyce   Brian Murphy
Vanda Godsell
Peter Hughes   Sue Bond
Rosanne Wickes

"SONGS FROM THE SHOWS"
John Hanson
Pamela Field   Ken Phillips Trio

"ONCE UPON A SOOTY TIME"
Barry Craine with Maxie Sparkle

Playhouse Theatre
WESTON-SUPER-MARE
Basil Flavell (Stepham-Bell with Mark Furness)

"LET'S DO IT YOUR WAY"
Liza Goddard   Colin Baker
Simon Merrick
Beth Ellis   Dudley Owen

"TWO AND TWO MAKE SEX"
Henry McGee
Tessa Wyatt   Ian Lavender
Peter Byrne

Pavilion Theatre
WEYMOUTH
Peter Maddock (Stepham-Bell with Mark Furness)

"THE MATING GAME"
Trevor Bannister   Hilary Pritchard
Queenie Watts   Christopher Mitchell
Miranda Messenger

ALL STAR SUNDAY CONCERTS
MARTI CAINE
DICK EMERY
BERNI FLINT
VINCE HILL
HINGE & BRACKET
HARRY WORTH
THE WURZELS

ALL BOX OFFICE RECORDS BROKEN AT EACH VENUE

THEATRE ROYAL NOTTINGHAM

Proprietors: The City of Nottingham

THANK YOU:-

MR. KEN DODD and Supporting Company
MISS YOOTHA JOYCE, MR. BRIAN MURPHY and Supporting Cast of GEORGE & MILDRED
The Principals and Members of THE D'OYLY CARTE OPERA
COMPANY and KENT OPERA, MR. GEORGE MELLY

for your incredible achievements in surpassing all previous Box Office Records at the Theatre Royal since 1948.

This theatre looks forward to a season of continued success with the following attractions:

Weekly attractions:

LILAC TIME, THE DANNY LA RUE SHOW, GOLDEN YEARS OF MUSIC HALL, GODSPELL, BASIL BRUSH SHOW, PROSPECT AT THE OLD VIC, SADLER'S WELLS ROYAL BALLET, UNEXPECTED GUEST, HAIR, DONKEY'S YEARS, WELSH NATIONAL OPERA GLYNDEBOURNE OPERA COMPANY.

Concerts:

SALUTE TO SATCHMO, HINGE & BRACKET, CLODAGH ROGERS, PAM AYRES, THE STYLISTICS.

There are one or two available weeks during the autumn season and I look forward to hearing from companies with suitable attractions.

Barrie C. Stead, General Manager and Artistic Director

The Stage on 18th August 1978 noted that the performance at the Pier Theatre was "tailor-made to suit the television personalities." "Viewed purely as a play, it's a little thin in the story department and there are no prizes for guessing what happens next. But with Brian and Yootha given superb material with which to snipe at each other continually, few give any thought to the plot but just sit back and rock with laughter. Yootha Joyce has the best of the barbs, which she launches at poor Brian, constantly reminding him of his lack of prowess in the love stakes. He defends himself as best he can, scoring points every now and then." *DEAR YOOTHA… THE LIFE OF YOOTHA JOYCE*

A day in the life of George and Mildred.....

The day began as usual. Mildred withdrew herself reluctantly from the arms of Gregory Peck and switched off the jangling alarm clock. George slept on, a little smile playing on his lips, his moustache twitching with pleasure as he dreamed he was flying about in heaven with his dear departed budgie, Oscar.

Mildred looked down at him tenderly. He wasn't Gregory Peck but at least he was there in the flesh, for what it was worth.

"Move over, George" said Mildred.

George moved over.

"No, towards ME, George."

George was out of bed like a streak of lightning. "I've just remembered, Mildred. It's my turn to make the tea."

Mildred sighed, relaxed back on the pillows and reflected on their 24 years together. She remembered all the little things, like the way George used to bite her thumb with his gums while they were at the pictures. She'd married him on the rebound, of course, when the G.I. she was engaged to went back to America and promised to send for her but never did. Stupid of me, thought Mildred, I should have remembered to give him my address. George's proposal had been direct and to the point. "My rubber hot water bottle's perished, Mildred, so why don't we get married to save me buying a new one."

Dear old George, he wasn't such a bad stick. And she'd had 24 years to get used to him. In 24 years you can get used to anything.

George interrupted her reminiscences with a tray of tea.

"You know, George", said Mildred. "I've got a touch of nostalgia this morning".

"I'll get you some disprin," said George.

After breakfast George sat reading page 3 of the Sun. Today's attraction was a well-developed Swedish blonde called Ingrid who had ambitions to become an Olympic sprinter. "She can chase me any time she likes," said George, chuckling at his own joke.

Mildred was busy clearing out a trunk. "Look George", she said "isn't this your old camera? It must be suffering from disuse atrophy. You can't have used it since we were in Dunkirk on our honeymoon."

"It's funny, I was just thinking about that, Mildred. The camera, I mean," said George, his eyes still glued to page 3. "I think I ought to go in for photography again. I had a lot of success at it as a youngster. Spent all me pocket money on films and flash bulbs. I remember they used to call me Flasher the Great."

"You could have fooled me," said Mildred.

George put Swedish Ingrid down till later and took the camera from Mildred. "I think I'll get cracking straightaway. I'll start off by taking a few snaps of the lads down at the British Legion, they'll like that. Can you lend me 50p for a film?"

"I'll GIVE you 50p. Then you'll still only owe me that £12 and the money you took out of the holiday box last week," sighed Mildred.

George bought his film, got the chemist to load it for him and popped into the pub for a quick pint. Next to him at the bar sat a young man with several cameras slung over his shoulder.

"Snap", said George, indicating his Kodak Brownie.

The young man smiled.

"You a photographer, too, then?" asked George.

The young man nodded.

"Are you a local fellow?" said George.

"Sort of," replied the young man. "I've got a studio opposite Hampton Court." He pushed his tankard away and stood up. "Must be off. I've got to do some shots for a girlie magazine this morning. Mustn't keep the model waiting".

"Oooooh!" said George. "Are you going to . . . I mean, will she . . . well, you know, be wearing a rude dress?"

"No," replied the young man, "It's all nude stuff. So long".

George asked for another pint to stop his head from swimming. By the time he got to the British Legion it was starting to drizzle. There was a girl sheltering in the doorway. George did a double-take. She was either Ingrid from page 3 or a close relative. George jumped as the girl suddenly darted towards him, her arms outstretched. "Thank goodness," she cried, "I'm . . ." George turned tail for home. After all, a photograph was something nice and artistic, but who needed the real thing?

"Please . . ." called the girl, hurrying after him. "I want you . . ."

George broke into a trot, not daring to look back over his shoulder.

The girl's feet kept tap-tapping behind him. He started to run, and could hear the girl running after him. George puffed on until he reached the safety of No. 46 Peacock Crescent. Only after he'd shut the gate firmly behind him did he turn round and look at the girl. Her thin dress was now very damp and clinging tightly to her body. Yes, she was definitely Ingrid from page 3.

"Look here," pleaded George. "I didn't mean what I said this morning about wanting you to chase me. You ought to know better, a big girl like you." The girl looked puzzled. "But I only want you to tell me where is Hampton Court please," she explained. "You see, a photographer is going to take my pictures, but I am so lost and running late on time. You looked such a kind man I was sure you would help me . . . like, like . . . St. George of Merrie England".

"How did you know me name?" asked George suspiciously. He did feel rather chuffed, though, and he was securely on home ground now. "I'll tell you what. Hampton Court's too far to walk in this weather. I'll ring for a taxi if you like.

"Oh, thank you," said the girl. "And while you are doing it perhaps I may dry off a little in your bath towel and use your toilette?"

George was torn between chivalry and doubt. "Mildred won't like it, but all right. I'll say you're my long lost second cousin from Australia."

Mildred was lying on the bed with her hair in rollers, her face white and stiff under a beauty mask, when she heard George's key in the door and then his voice calling her name. No point in replying and cracking the now firmly-set face mask. She kept silent.

"That's a relief," said George. "She must be out. Now get a move on. It's up the stairs and first on the right."

Five minutes later Ingrid emerged in a dry dress she'd been carrying in her handbag, just as the taxi George had ordered drew up at the front door.

"How can I thank you?" she said, and kissed George on the cheek.

"Hey, none of that," said George.

"Perhaps you would like to take my photograph some time?" whispered Ingrid, and slipped a piece of paper into his hand. George looked down at it. It was a phone number. When he looked up, the taxi was carrying Ingrid off and she was blowing kisses at him through the window.

He was still in a daze when Mildred came downstairs, her beauty treatment completed. "I thought I heard voices," she said. "Have we had visitors?"

"Only my long lost second cousin from Australia," George told her. "She just wanted to spend a penny, then she had to be off again."

"Wasn't it rather a long way to come just for that?" asked Mildred as she started laying the table.

"Well, you know me," said George. "Can't stand my relatives. Well, I mean, you don't want strangers walking all over your home, do you?"

After supper that evening, Mildred went back to clearing the old trunk and George sat reading page 3 again. He was grinning from ear to ear.

"You seem very pleased with yourself, George," said Mildred. "Like you'd just won the Cup for England single-handed."

George tapped the photograph of Ingrid with his hand. "See this girl, Mildred? Well, I met her this morning."

"Did you, George?" Might as well humour him, thought Mildred.

"Yes, she asked me if I'd like to take some pictures of her."

"Did she, George?"

"I told her I was a bit busy"

"Of course, George."

"But she insisted on leaving me her phone number."

"Ex-directory, of course, George".

"She called me St. George of Merrie England. Hee-hee!"

"George, have you got a temperature? I think you'd better have an early night".

"What about you, Mildred?"

"It'll take me at least an hour to finish sorting this trunk".

"Good. I mean, good idea of yours about me having an early night. I'll go on up, then."

George was fast asleep when Mildred crept in beside him. He was dreaming that he was back with Oscar, only this time Oscar was perched on his shoulder while he, the country's most sought-after photographer, took pictures of a blonde beauty queen. "Drop the towel a bit, Ingrid," muttered George in his sleep, "That's better. Now . . . watch the birdie!" Mildred looked at him and shook her head. She'd get the doctor if he wasn't better in the morning. Then she noticed he was clutching a little piece of paper. She unscrewed it, but it was just a phone number. "Poor George," thought Mildred. "He's really carrying his fantasies to the limit, writing down imaginary phone numbers from imaginary girls." She tore the paper up into little fragments, kissed George on his forehead, turned over and shut her eyes. All was well with the world. Gregory Peck was waiting.

"I think she had had enough of playing Mildred after about a year. - She got a bit depressed after playing Mildred for a while. Nothing else was being offered, and that was a problem. It's sad but it happens still to so many actors." **TERENCE LEE DICKSON**

Yootha at the Durrell wildlife trust in Jersey.

The trust's honorary director, Lee Durrell, told me her visit in 1978 was organized by the then Trust Secretary, Simon Hicks. The trust's zoological director in those days was Jeremy Mallinson: he said he was "most impressed by her very sincere and keen interest in the animal kingdom. It was not a question of a person showing mild interest, she was obviously emotionally attached to the Trust. She was a genuine and nice person." "She joined its animal adoption scheme and helped in fund-raising events." DEAR YOOTHA... THE LIFE OF YOOTHA JOYCE

"I think she would have liked to reduce her work load, perhaps open a donkey sanctuary. Also, spend time in Spain for maybe six months of the year. I got the feeling that if somebody could have persuaded her to do these things she would have given them a try. She was also fond of a relaxed lifestyle." TERENCE LEE DICKSON

Yootha in the arms of Tom Jones.
Image Courtesy Viv Jones.

Peter Frazer Jones remarked that "Yootha had become painfully thin, and was quite withdrawn, and sometimes, if I wandered down onto the studio floor in the lunch break, I would find her there, sitting quite alone and rather sad." This sadness was doubtless due to the breakdown of Yootha's relationship with Terry Lee Dickson. She later said: "at long last I can say: we'll thank God that's ended. We would have destroyed each other." DEAR YOOTHA… THE LIFE OF YOOTHA JOYCE

"I don't feel I own anybody, and nobody must feel they own me." YOOTHA JOYCE

"I know she would have been shattered at the breakup. How it happened I have no idea but she just told me at some time that Terry had found someone else. Whether that's how it really happened I don't know. I only know what I was told." JOY JAMESON

"There came a time when I sat down and realised there would come a time when the age differences, instead of bringing us closer, would become more separated. We were together for a relatively short period of time." TERENCE LEE DICKSON

"Yootha was such a genuine open loving giving person essentially, that if she didn't get it back, and very often people couldn't, she did feel let down. I think that what she needed would have been an older man to look after her, but that's not what she looked for." ADRIANNE HAMILTON

Work & Performance Highlights 1979

George & Mildred (TV)
Series 5 Episodes
24/10/79   Finders Keepers?
30/10/79   In Sickness & in Health
06/11/79   The Last Straw
13/11/79   A Driving Ambition
27/11/79   A Military Pickle
04/12/79   Fishy Business
18/12/79   I Gotta Horse
25/12/79   The Twenty-six Year Itch
Role - Mildred Roper

Eric Morecambe's £100 sketch.
Going — Gone!

PHILLIPS, the London Fine Art auctioneers, beat their last year's record by raising close on £5,000 for the Stars' Organisation for Spastics (SOS). For sale by auction at their Blenheim Street premises were 80 lots featuring some of the most unexpected artists' names ever to appear in a Phillips Fine Art catalogue.

Clive Dunn who organised the event, contributed Lot 68, a portrait of Sir John Mills, retiring chairman of SOS. Clive not only painted it, he sold it for £110.

Anthony Quayle, who takes over this year as Chairman of the Stars' Organisation in succession to Mills, auctioned an artist's proof of himself as King Lear by New Statesman cartoonist Ralph Steadman. It fetched £105.

The joint managing director of Phillips, Christopher Hawkings, handled the gavel for the most part himself — when such formidable female talents as Yootha Joyce and Joan Turner permitted during the hilarious two-hour session. He knocked down a chalk drawing by Eric Morecambe for £100 and cajoled excellent prices for uncatalogued doodles and cartoons by Bob Monkhouse and Max Bygraves.

"I remember one evening after filming we were all having a meal in the restaurant at the Thames Studios in Teddington with all the cast and crew, and I didn't like most of what was on the menu, so Yootha (who I was sitting next to) asked me what I wanted if I could have anything, so I said I would really like a banana and honey sandwich! So she asked the waiter for some bread, butter and honey and then got a banana from the fruit bowl and proceeded to slice the banana up and make me a sandwich in front of everyone, just to make me happy; that's the kind of person she was and I still miss her to this day! It was a long time ago but I can still remember a lot of it, as it was such a special time in my life!"
NICHOLAS BOND OWEN

George & Mildred. (THEATRE)
Stage show UK / Australasian Tour. Johnnie Mortimer & Brian Cooke
Role - Mildred Roper

"We were taken to Australia and New Zealand: the plans were being finalised. It was incredible: there was no time for anything else, we were asked individually to do other types of plays, but we had to decline. We lived and breathed George and Mildred." BRIAN MURPHY

London-Frankfurt
1hr 20mins

Refreshment

Danish open sandwiches

French apple pie

In flight menu and schedule to Australia, which Yootha kept.

Frankfurt-Rome
1hr 40mins

Light Meal

Lobster à la Nage
Potato & green salad
Green Goddess dressing

Fruit salad

Roll & butter

Coffee-Tea

Rome-Bahrain
4hrs 50mins

Dinner

Hors d'oeuvre Silver Kris

Paupiette of veal à la grecque
Home made noodle
French beans in brown butter
Stuffed tomato with pineapple

Chicken sauté à la lyonnaise
Duchess potatoes
French beans in brown butter
Creamed mushrooms

Budapest pineapple Torte

Cheese & crackers

Roll & butter

Coffee - Tea

Bahrain-Bombay
3hrs 10mins

Breakfast

Chilled orange juice

Fruit appetiser

Cereal

Grilled lamb cutlet
Grilled tomato
Sauté mushrooms

Marinated deep fat fried fish
Hashed potatoes
Grilled tomato

Croissant
Brioche

Butter - Marmalade

Coffee - Tea

Bombay-Singapore
5hrs 05mins

Light Meal

Mixed green salad

Grilled lobster tail
Stuffed potatoes
Creamed mushrooms
Broccoli braised in wine

Chocolate profiteroles

Roll & butter

Coffee - Tea

Singapore-Perth
4hrs. 50 mins.

Dinner

Hors d'oeuvre Silver Kris

Fillet of beef Prince Albert
Noisette potatoes
Broccoli braised in wine
Stuffed tomato with diced pineapple

Stir-fried chicken in
    oyster sauce
Rice pilaf
Stir-fried cauliflower
    & mushrooms
Green peas & mint

Peach cream torte

Cheese & crackers

Roll & butter

Coffee-Tea

Perth-Melbourne
3hrs. 20 mins.

Breakfast

Chilled orange juice

Fruit appetiser

Cereal

Grilled fillet steak
Grilled tomato
Sauté mushrooms

Marinated fillets of sole
Hashed potatoes
Grilled tomato

Croissant
Brioche

Butter-Marmalade

Coffee-Tea

"The trip was: London to Frankfurt, Frankfurt to Rome, Rome to Bahrain, Bahrain to Bombay, Bombay to Singapore, Singapore to Perth, Perth to Melbourne – then onto New Zealand, certainly a challenge even to anyone who enjoys flying!"
Brian recalled that on the flight to New Zealand, and the others that were to follow, Yootha loathed it." He remembered that, though they arrived safely, "our costumes didn't. We were late by one day, and with a total sell-out at the theatre; being a day late, we were missing a day of acclimatising and adjusting to the time differences. The temperature was really hot and humid. We were on stage doing our first show to a lovely audience, and suddenly we stopped, and for a split second we had no idea where we were; we got through it. We were jet-lagged." *DEAR YOOTHA... THE LIFE OF YOOTHA JOYCE*

Yootha and Brian stayed at various locations during the tour. On one occasion they stayed at the White Heron Hotel, Auckland, which had small apartments, overlooking the ocean. In Bruce: The Autobiography *Bruce Forsyth recalled staying at the same hotel, with both Yootha and Brian, at the same time. It was "one of the longest birthdays of my life," he says, and describes them both as the "most fun-loving people, with great senses of humour. When Yootha found out it was my birthday, she organised an impromptu get-together the night before. We sat by the pool at the White Heron under a starlit sky, eating fish and chips – served with champagne – waiting for me to turn 47." DEAR YOOTHA… THE LIFE OF YOOTHA JOYCE*

Yootha hated flying and she always used to sit next to me and dig her fingernails into my arm during the takeoff and landing. She was quite scared. I used to ask her if I could sit by the window, not to look at the view, but to spare my left arm and let my right one get some punishment. I went round with these big gouges in my arm for days afterwards!
BRIAN MURPHY

Some of the postcards Yootha kept from her visit to Australasia.

The 21st Annual TV Week Logie Awards (TV)
[Australia]
Role - Herself

Ten Celebrity Interviews (TV) [Australia]
Role – Herself

Ten Townsville News (TV) [Australia]
Role – Herself

The Mike Walsh Show (TV) [Australia]
- Episode 9139
Role – Herself

At **The Canberra Times,** *Yootha stressed that "there are millions of George and Mildreds, and they are trying to identify with you every minute of the day." She also said that "it has its good sides, my bank manager is awfully pleased with me, but it gets a bit trying sometimes, you tend to live in a goldfish bowl, everybody looks points pokes and shoves, but loads and loads of nice things come out of it too." DEAR YOOTHA… THE LIFE OF YOOTHA JOYCE*

"I love cards… and gambling, I like going to the races, the dogs and playing roulette. But I've never really had a big win. My biggest winnings are in the £20 to £30 range" YOOTHA JOYCE

"Yootha loved the horses. And she'd dress to the nines for a day at the races, that was right up her alley." CHRISTINE PILGRIM

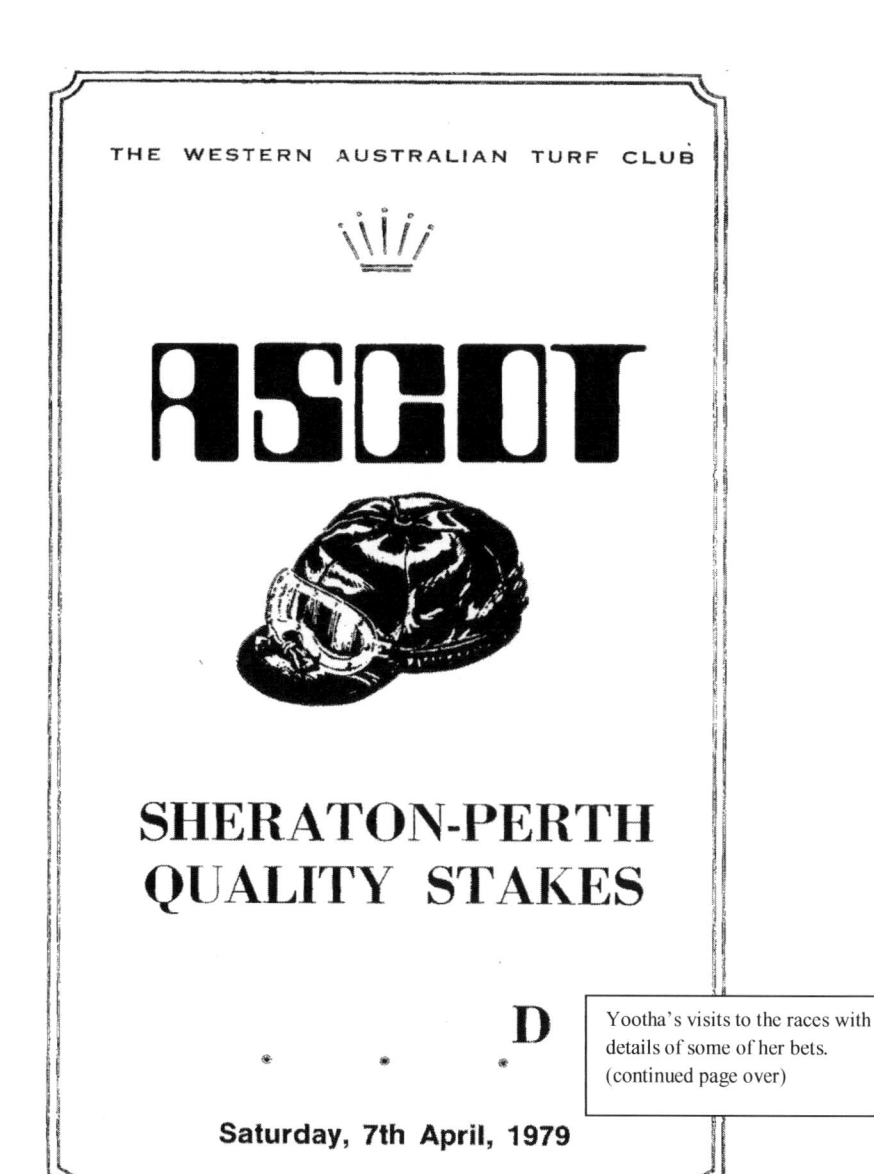

Yootha's visits to the races with details of some of her bets. (continued page over)

Double: This and the next: Races 6 & 7.

6 Sheraton-Perth Quality Stakes 4.25

1. HAKIM BOY — 57.5
Dr. H. J. Melville, J. V. Quackenbush & A. List
(K. W. Leaver)
B.c. 2 Jungle Boy (GB)—Towerwyn Opn (191:1) - - 1 1
DARK BLUE and pink diamonds, dark blue cap
Barrier 9   GERRY DONNELLY

①ⁿᵈ Win

2. LATIN SAINT — 55.0
J. & Mrs J. Sarich & G. Wickham (A. N. Hawke)
B.c. 2 Le Cordonnier (GB)—Othelia Trl (196:1) - - 1
BLACK and white diamonds, black sleeves, quartered cap
Barrier 4   GLEN DAVIES

②

3. CHESS KING — 52.5
G. & Mrs G. Wickham & J. L. & Mrs J. L. Sarich
(P. G. Rock)
B.c. 2 King Of Babylon (Ire)—Chess Mate Enc (196:2) - - 1 1
LILAC, black hoops and cap
Barrier 2   LINDSAY RUDLAND

③

4. JUNGLE ROYAL — 49.0
Mrs J. S. Aramini (J. S. Aramini)
Ch.g. 2 Jungle Boy (GB)—Royal Pink Adv (199:1) T3 1p1p
ORANGE, lilac sleeves and cap
Barrier 6   ROD KEMP

Win

5. BORN REGAL — 48.5
A. W. & A. R. Williams & R. W. Rayment
(R. W. Rayment)
B.c. 2 Zvornik—Vyanje Imp (193:2) 6p0 0 1p
TANGERINE, dark blue sleeves and cap
Barrier 8   MARK SESTICH¶

Place

6. GIVEN VISION — 48.5
A. H. Gilbert, Mrs J. B. W. & J. B. W. Court,
B. L. Harvey & R. J. Wilberforce (A. H. Jordan)
Ch.f. 2 Approval (GB)—Decameron Tran (196:1) - - - 3
WHITE, red maltese cross, armbands and cap
Barrier 12   DANNY MILLER

Place

7. ANDY'S CHOICE (B) — 48.0
D. P. & Mrs D. P. & D. S. J. & Mrs D. S. J. Lawler
(D. P. Lawler)
B.c. 2 Zvornik—School Lamp Imp (200:1) 4p7 6 5
PURPLE and yellow diamonds and yellow cap
Barrier 5   RUSSELL STEWART*

8. BLUE TILLA — 48.0
Mesdames M. E. Taylor & R. J. Sweetapple
(Mrs M. E. Taylor)
Gr.g. 2 Croft What's Wanted (GB)—Arbotilla
Mdn (196:2) - - 8 6
DARK BLUE and yellow quarters, quartered cap
Barrier 3   MARK GRIGSBY‡

9. CHIMING STAR — 48.0
N. A. & Mrs N. A. Parnham (R. C. McPherson)
Blk.c. 2 Chiming (NZ)—Lady Martone Mdn (196:1) T2T7 0
GREEN, purple striped sleeves, hooped cap
Barrier 14   HARRY WULFF

10. GREAT PARTHENON — 48.0
A. & Mrs A. Pitsikas (R. R. Marlow)
B.c. 2 Just Great (GB)—Amparo Mdn (196:2) - - 8
LIGHT BLUE, purple armbands and cap
Barrier 10   GRAEME WEBSTER (Jnr.)¶

11. PETERSEN — 48.0
R. C. & Mrs R. C. McPherson (R. C. McPherson)
Ch.g. 2 Gay Saba (NZ)—Rawson mare Mdn * T7T8
PINK, brown sash, light blue armbands and cap
Barrier 1   STEPHEN MILLER*

12. TODVEGA — 48.0
K. G. Williamson (R. H. Treffone)
B.c. 2 Zvornik—Pastel Lady Mdn (196:2) - 3
YELLOW, black sash, quartered cap
Barrier 7   GRAHAM LAMBIE

13. WESTERN SYMBOL — 48.0
Archie Martin & Sons Syndicate (A. R. Martin)
B.c. 2 Biscay—Mareega Mdn (196:1) T4T2 9 9
PURPLE, light blue spots and cap
Barrier 11   MERV POSNER

14. ZEN — 48.0
Sir Ernest Lee-Steere & J. H. O'Halloran
(R. O. Meyers)
B.f. 2 Zvornik—Astra Vista Mdn (191:1) T3 2p5p6
ALL RED
Barrier 13   DANNY HOBBY*

HAKIM BOY — LATIN SAINT — CHESS KING

ABBREVIATIONS

The classification of each horse is shown before the horse's form.

Mdn	— Maiden		Nov	— Novice ($1,200)
Imp	— Improvers ($300)		Tran	— Transition ($1,300)
Prog	— Progressive ($350)		Enc	— Encourage ($1,450)
Int	— Intermediate ($400)		Trl	— Trial ($1,650)
Adv	— Advanced ($450)		Opn	— Open

APPRENTICES ALLOWANCES

RUDLAND D.	nil	WEBSTER G. (Jnr.)	1.5
SESTICH M.	1.5	BUNTING G.	2.5
YOUNG D.	1.5	GRIGSBY M.	2.5

All other apprentices may claim 3.0kg.

Give Us a Clue (TV)
2 Episodes
Role – Herself

"The ever moving predatory hands are softly lit with topaz and gold rings. Her boobs are as pointed as her teeth, and she is deathly sexy. She has eyelashes like poisonous spiders. Her mouth is vast and luscious, like a gaping sea-anemone. Or Jaws, or a mail box. Or the red hole. Or a cave filled with what looks like 132 jagged pearl teeth. To men, the mouth, which could kiss or tell, or even kill you, is irresistible. To realise the true size and power of it, you have to see it in the gleaming pink flesh. Even without a tape, I'd work it out at a third again as wide as Sophia Loren's and twice Farrah Fawcett-Majors'. It's more than a gap in her face, it is a geological marvel." JEAN ROOK

Radio 1 Roadshow (RADIO)
Role – Herself

ON Monday of this week nine Pye Colour Television Awards, given in association with the Writers' Guild, were presented at the Hilton Hotel in London.

Thames's The Plank, written and directed by Eric Sykes, was judged the Best Written Comedy Contribution of the year, and the award was presented to Eric by Bill Oddie.

The Most Promising New Writer award went to Victoria Wood, for her play Talent, which although originally a stage play was recorded in studio by Granada. Joanna Lumley made the presentation.

Richard Cooper won the Children's Writer of the Year award for his script for Tyne Tees, A Quest of Eagles. This award was presented by Jenny Hanley.

The award for the Best Female Comedy Role Created for Television by a Writer went to Leonard Webb for the roles of Maggie and Mrs Perry, in London Weekend's Maggie and Her. Julia McKenzie and Irene Handl, who play the two ladies, also received an award — Irene Handl's first — and Yootha Joyce made the presentation.

Judith Chalmers presented the award for Regional Colour Production which this year was won by Westward for The Gibsons of Scilly, a documentary produced by John Bartlett.

Denis Norden was named as Outstanding Male Personality for presenting LWT's It'll Be Alright on the Night and Thames's Looks Familiar, while Barbara Woodhouse won the Outstanding Female Personality award for her BBC-2 series, Training

MILD. BUT NOT MEEK.

Three Fives Medium Mild

More betting details for a greyhound meeting at White City.

LOW TO MIDDLE TAR Manufacturer's estimate
H.M. Government Health Departments' WARNING:
CIGARETTES CAN SERIOUSLY DAMAGE YOUR HEALTH

TVTimes STAR EVENING in aid of "OLD BEN" (NEWSVENDORS' BENEVOLENT INSTITUTION)

CHARITY GREYHOUND MEETING WHITE CITY STADIUM

Tuesday 9th October 1979 at 7·45pm

Yootha was now having some trouble with Mildred. In a later interview she admitted to having "a scorching temper and a lava tongue, which would get her into boiling water with her fans," "I loathe being touched, I can't stand grabbers who come up to you in the street and literally shake your shoulders. The way they grab and shake and shout at you tells you 'I OWN you, you belong to me" DEAR YOOTHA... THE LIFE OF YOOTHA JOYCE

Work & Performance Highlights 1980

George & Mildred (FILM)
Role - Mildred Roper

"I do get tired of Mildred. I love her and I'm grateful for what she has done for me, sometimes I think if I see Mildred written down one more time I'll scream." YOOTHA JOYCE

"I won't give up Mildred so long as the viewers like her." YOOTHA JOYCE

"I know it happens to other actors, but George and Mildred are especially hard to live with, much as we have loved the work. Consider it - the middle-aged wife, deeply fond of a middle-aged husband, who can't make love to her, and who gets on her wick. She'd never leave him, she'd be desolate without him, and anyway, what are they going to do apart? But he still drives her berserk. Can't you see, after all these years of doing it, it's hard to take? I'm ashamed of myself for letting Mildred get me down off screen." YOOTHA JOYCE

Though the TV ratings remained very high, even Yootha, Brians Murphy and Cooke and Johnnie Mortimer knew the script ideas were starting to become, as Yootha said, "a little stale." "There was," Yootha admitted, a "deliberate attempt to stop, as the writers are finding less situations for us as characters." The new film script featuring the Ropers was toasted up by a different writer, Dick Sharples. There was also a further promise of a final set of TV scripts in preparation by Cooke and Mortimer, who by now seemed to be focused on devising newer material and formats. DEAR YOOTHA…
THE LIFE OF YOOTHA JOYCE

"I never did see the George and Mildred movie, but then I think I'd find it a bit difficult to watch. Various series are shown from time to time and I choose not to watch them. I have a gorgeous memory of those days and I don't want to spoil that.
I remember her being perfect,, perfect, not good, perfect, such a level of skill, commitment at times, frighteningly good."
TERENCE LEE DICKSON

Yootha on set of the *George and Mildred* film at Elstree. Also photographed outside the Copthorne Tara Hotel, London, publicising the film.

Give Us a Clue (TV)
2 Episodes
Role – Herself
(2nd episode Broadcast 24 August 1980)

"I can't do anything else now, people just won't give you the work, I can't be considered as a straight actress any more on television. I think I'll have to wait for a little while before it eases off and then do all sorts of other things; we have another eight more George and Mildred's to do and then we finish." Tony Bilbow, who was an admirer, asked about doing other projects that would stretch her as an actress. She said: "It would be easy to do in the theatre, but the thing is, I just love working in television." DEAR YOOTHA… THE LIFE OF YOOTHA JOYCE

"Yootha wanted to break into more serious acting." Christine Pilgrim thought, *"Once Mildred had taken over Yootha's life, she held out little hope that she'd be cast as anything else. She found the character rather two-dimensional, although she did everything she could to round Mildred out. And she succeeded as far as anyone can with a sitcom character. I think she was more frustrated with becoming public property as Mildred. She couldn't go to the supermarket without people addressing her as Mildred. It was as if they owned her. She was part of their lives, so they presumed they could be part of hers. She had no privacy any more. I think that was very wearing for her. She stopped going shopping, or at least did as little of it as possible."* There were regular repeats of the problems of being recognised in the street, in which she said *"people often come up to me and ask the most embarrassing questions about Mildred's sex life."* It was frustrating for her. She said, *"I had, before Mildred, established myself firmly as an equally accomplished dramatic actress."* DEAR YOOTHA… THE LIFE OF YOOTHA JOYCE

"I don't remember that awful wallpaper!" **TERENCE LEE DICKSON**

Yootha at home and attending her friends' wedding.

"I am a hard critic; I have never been satisfied with my performances on or off stage." **YOOTHA JOYCE**

In 1980 she said: "A journalist described me once as 'a lady of wit and maturity who, in the Edwardian age, would have had young swains drinking champagne out of her size eight slipper and ordering many an intimate dinner à deux in the red plush private rooms of certain discreet restaurants.' Dudley Sutton saw things differently, saying she was "Deluded, yes, Yootha started seeing herself as a sort of grand lady, a charitable lady, with large hats hanging in front of pillars, serving tea in the garden! She had kind of lost the plot." DEAR YOOTHA… THE LIFE OF YOOTHA JOYCE

"Rosy and I had all our wedding photos scanned recently, and here's one of Yootha with us as she adjusts my tie for me, We were married on 17th April 1980 and she died just four months later. I have very fond memories of her at our wedding." FABIAN HAMILTON

"I didn't see Yootha for several months after the Australia trip: "I thought she was happily resting, but she was just staying at home getting more and more lonely and miserable. The trouble was she didn't have many close friends and she didn't go out much. I was horrified when I did see Yootha again after the several months away; she had become painfully thin and I should have interfered. I should have tried to help her. Being Yootha, she would have told me to fuck off, but I still should have said something to her and I didn't."   BRIAN MURPHY

On August 6th, Yootha collapsed after contracting a chronic liver infection: she weighed just under seven stone. She agreed to enter a Harley Street clinic: when she was admitted she was disturbed and distressed when she was told she could no longer drink, and a psychiatrist specialising in alcohol problems was called as "she was suffering from hepatitis." Joy (Jameson) thought that Yootha had initially gone into hospital with what she thought was a "chest infection, as she had a dreadful cough. She was always coughing and I did nag her to get it looked at in case it was anything nasty. It wouldn't have surprised me if they had come back with a cancer diagnosis. She was underweight and getting feeble (that's not the word I want, but you know, you wonder if she had to be careful because she certainly wasn't herself). I truly believed they would sort her out in time. You certainly don't expect someone to go in with something you think is curable." DEAR YOOTHA… THE LIFE OF YOOTHA JOYCE

It was reported on 22nd August that doctors at the clinic thought she was on the mend. Two days earlier, on her 53rd birthday, Brian Murphy recalled, "she was sitting up in bed, surrounded by hundreds of flowers and cards from fans and the press and it looked like she was improving. The Sun reported 'On her birthday she received 800 cards and telegrams at the hospital.' That bucked her up immensely." On Sunday 24th, he went over to the hospital. "I had gone to visit my own dear mum and I was on the way back home, when I decided to pay Yootha a visit instead. She went into a coma as I was there. It was a great shock. But she had a relapse and slipped away literally while I was sitting there. It was so very sad.
When I first met her, she seemed to know exactly where she was headed. Trouble with being an actor, we can sometimes fool our friends and ourselves." DEAR YOOTHA… THE LIFE OF YOOTHA JOYCE

In the early seventies Yootha Joyce made appearances in the BBC's Jimmy Tarbuck series, Tarbuck's Luck, and in London Weekend's The Fenn Street Gang, before Thames's Man About the House brought her the role of Mildred, playing opposite Brian Murphy's George. After five series of Man About the House, Thames gave them their own series, George and Mildred, in 1976.

The company had planned a further series of the programme, to be made when Yootha Joyce recovered, despite the fact that speaking to Television Today some time ago, Yootha Joyce had said she would complete the George and Mildred film but make no further episodes.

The series will be remembered as one of those of which even repeat showings could win peak-time audiences and appear in the ratings.

The last recording that Yootha Joyce made was for an edition of Thames's charade game, Give Us a Clue, which she had recorded earlier in the year and which Thames showed on Monday of this week.

Yootha's final resting place: The Crocus Lawn (Plot 3P) at Golders Green Crematorium. London.

"She had so much to give and should have had more time to show the public what a great actress she was," **JEREMY BULLOCH (CO-ACTOR)**

"I keep a beautiful necklace Yootha gave me - a Maltese cross which a lot of people say is the cross of the Mafia?! I think of her often. I can't think of anyone who had a bad word to say about her." **JOY JAMESON**

"Her death came as quite a shock to me, to people in show business and to the millions of viewers who loved her. Since her death I have been touched by the amazing amount of mail I have received from viewers who regarded us as man and wife. They came from people who were genuinely upset. - Of course I miss her; we were more than friends - we were great mates. I know Yootha would have wanted me to get back into situation comedy, just as I would have wished her to do the same had the tragedy happened to me." **BRIAN MURPHY**

"On her death the press were banging on the door of the theatre in Glasgow I was working in. I remember I was working on some lighting aspects of a performance when some cleaner left the door open. Suddenly the press got in and rushed to the foot of the stage. I was then blinded by a series of flashes, which kind of ruined my vision in a way. My stage crew got to the front of the stage and er, well, helped them out, quite quickly. Unfortunately for them, someone had closed the doors in front of them!" **TERENCE LEE DICKSON**

Post 1980

Yootha's Posthumous Broadcasts

'Max '(TV)
Appearing as herself and singing the song For All We Know with host Max Bygraves
14/01/81

Funny You Should Ask (RADIO)
"*Peter Jones puts the questions and Les Dawson, Dickie Henderson and Yootha Joyce provide the answers and reminiscences, (Recorded before an invited audience in 1980)*"
03/03/81

Dear Yootha...

Paul Curran

The Life of Yootha Joyce

BUY NOW
amazon.co.uk